THE UPPER HAND

THE UPPER HAND

Leveraging Limitations to Turn Adversity into Advantage

CHRIS RUDEN

The Upper Hand: Leveraging Limitations to Turn Adversity into Advantage

Editor: Christine Gordon Manley

Developmental Editor: Jaime Lee Mann

Book Designer: Jamie Arts

Published in Stratford, Canada, by Blue Moon Publishers. Printed and bound in Canada.

ISBN: 978-1-989517-49-9

CONTENTS

To my fellow Type 1 Diabetics, limb different people, amputees, and anyone who lives with struggles they never asked for.

ACKNOWLEDGEMENTS

I want to thank everyone who made fun of me for the way I was born and put limits on my ability to ever be more than the kid wearing the glove. You all showed me limits I needed to break, and without your misplaced judgements, I might not have gotten to this place in my life or have ever written this book. Because of you, I've learned that, regardless of how cruel people can be, we all have the ability to develop a strong sense of inner self-worth while focusing on effective thinking and blocking out the noise. Because of you, thousands of people will finally hear the words they've needed to hear for so long.

So thank you again, not for what you said or did, but for providing me with what I needed so that I could build off of your mistakes and better myself.

MY STORY

A threshold guardian is someone or something standing between a hero and their goal. In every classic story, the threshold guardian tests the hero's resolve and threatens their journey. For Luke Skywalker, the threshold guardian was the storm troopers. For Oedipus, it was the Sphinx.

At a first glance, the threshold guardian *seems* like the biggest hurdle that the hero faces. But at the end of the day, it's not the threshold guardian that's the problem. The real problem is the hero's perception of that problem.

For many years, my threshold guardian was my hand.

I was born with a congenital birth defect that gave me a shorter left arm and three missing fingers. I viewed my disability as the thing that was standing in my way of everything I ever wanted. But my hand wasn't stopping me from anything. I was stopping me from fully accepting myself the way that I was.

You may think your threshold guardian is your gender, your socio-economic status, your weight, your boss, your disease... but is it really?

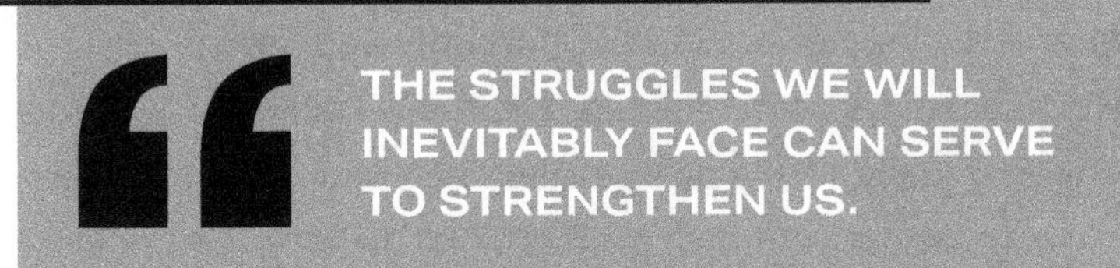

This book is not a memoir. I will only use my story to carry examples throughout the different topics I write about. But there are some key details that you should know.

My life was going pretty well when I was a kid... until middle school, when a girl I had a crush on made fun of my hand in front of everyone in our class and called me Claw Boy.

I kept my hand in my pocket for years. In high school, I removed my hand from my pocket, only to cover it up with a glove. Then the glove became my crutch.

I was an angry teenager who made a lot of bad decisions that led me down a dangerous path. On that path, I found aggression, depression, rage, partying, drugs, alcohol... oh, and a diagnosis of Type 1 Diabetes at 19 years old, during my second semester of college.

Drugs were a part of my life from age 18 to 23. I should have died. When I was partying, people loved me. I was fun, and I had fun. I fit in, and I was able to forget the things I wanted to forget. I still hid my hand.

My whole life was lived around hiding my hand. Long sleeve shirts, holding doors a certain way, positioning myself so a date wouldn't notice my glove... It was exhausting.

In college, I found myself in a really bad place after a longterm relationship had ended, so I went to see a therapist. At the end of the session, the therapist gave me a card with a suicide hotline number on it. That was a wake-up call for me, and that's when I started to slowly take better care of myself. I started looking better and feeling better, and the partying died down.

I switched majors a ton of times, eventually landing on exercise science. Eventually, I became a certified personal trainer. (A great way to forget about your own problems, by the way, is by helping someone else.) But exercise became a career for me, and I loved it. Fitness, diabetes, and a mindset shift helped to save me from my own mental trauma. I became a speaker along the way, and now check it out: I've written a book.

My hope here is to arm you (ha ha) with the perspective I wish I had several years back.

I'm not perfect. I struggle. I still battle with depression from time to time. I have periods of funk. We need to allow those moments, get through them, and carry on. What's different for me now is that I've taught myself how to shift my perspective to ride out the lows. I'm still the guy that I was at 19. Same disability, same disease, same past. None of that changed, but my perspective did. I made it past the threshold guardian, and this book can help you do the same.

INTRODUCTION

Lemons are not a naturally occurring fruit. They're actually a hybrid, created by humans. That old saying, "When life gives you lemons, make lemonade" is pretty ironic because life didn't give anyone a lemon. We made the lemons ourselves.

> "AS HUMAN BEINGS, WE CREATE OUR OWN LEMONS.
>
> WE TEND TO EXACERBATE OUR OWN PROBLEMS.
>
> AND THAT IS THE WHOLE POINT OF THIS BOOK.

Did reading that make you feel uncomfortable? I get it. I've been in a place where I would have struggled to digest that statement, too. The concept that we create our own problems takes some getting used to.

Did I create my own physical disability? Did I create Type 1 Diabetes for myself? Did I eventually end up with addiction issues on purpose? No. Of course I didn't.

But who decided that any of those things (disability, diabetes, addiction) are negative? Everything in life is just data. Neutral data. We choose to assign a negative or positive value to something, depending on how we interpret the data. I believe the secret to having a good life is about where you put your focus. While I did not sign up for my physical conditions, I assigned myself a narrative that made them more difficult.

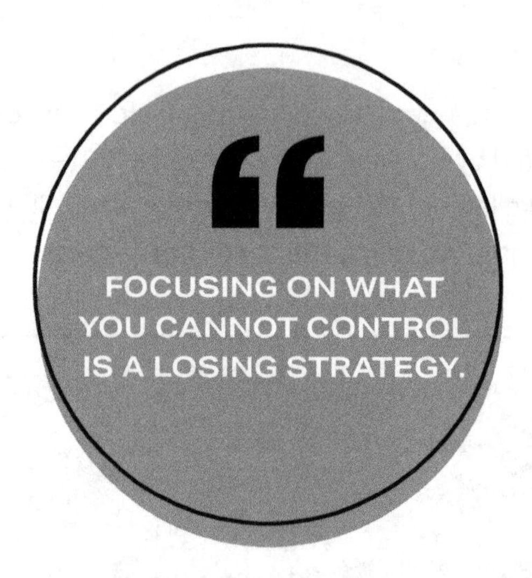

I wrote this book to try and help you get out of the same kinds of crappy thought patterns that I got myself out of by changing the way I look at things—changing the lemons I created for myself and changing how I interpreted the sourness of those lemons.

In life, things happen that we wouldn't necessarily sign up for. But it's not about what happens *to us* that's important. What's important is *what we do with* what happens to us.

Listen. Life will sling mud at you. Maybe even bricks. While some people believe that the mud and bricks are intentional and serve some purpose (i.e., "everything happens for a reason"), I believe things just... happen. And *we* apply reason to them.

Mud will be thrown, and if you get hit by it, well, that's unfortunate, but it isn't necessarily intended for you.

I don't believe that all things happen for a reason. Nobody is throwing anything at you; it's just happening. I know you might not like that I'm saying this. Especially if you take comfort in the philosophy that all things do happen for a reason. But bear with me because there is a cathartic freedom in randomness.

While some people may feel things happen because of a higher power, I fully believe in free will and the objective belief that the world around us is spontaneous and unguided. We are the intentional agents of change and creation or destruction of thoughts, beliefs, and actions, and we sometimes encounter unexpected happenings. As humans, our safety relies on our ability to interpret and respond to circumstances, which can be both to our benefit (positivity and effective thinking) and our detriment (negativity and ineffective thinking).

Having diabetes is just a fact for me. And it's outside of my control. Maybe it was genetic. Maybe it was my diet. Maybe I was destined to get it. Maybe... Maybe... Maybe... People drive themselves mad with what ifs and maybes, spending so much time coming up with possibilities and zero time on practicality and actual solutions. Humans have this weird habit of fantasizing about what if or why or maybe. This removes all of our power and removes us from the present.

People sit dormant in the present wishing for a different past in hopes of creating a better future. But a better future never comes from wishing about the past. It comes from taking advantage of the present.

We want to apply reason to things that happen because people love to believe in connectedness. We want to connect the dots—we *need* to connect the dots. The human brain is pattern-seeking and purpose-seeking as a survival mechanism to protect us in harmful scenarios. That behaviour carries over into the overly regurgitated "everything happens for a reason" quote.

We refuse to let the dots exist without a connection. If you draw a circle that's 99% complete, and ask someone to draw it, they'll draw a full circle because of an innate need to feel completion.

People want to know *the why*. Why is this happening? Why is this happening *to me*? But the why doesn't matter as much as what you do with it. The why does nothing for today.

Why care about the why (*why was I born this way? why wasn't I born into wealth?*)—something you can't control—when you can care about *the what* (*how can I use my disability to inspire other people? What can I do to create my own wealth?*)—something you can control?

Go from a *why me* to a *try me* attitude. Who cares if you're *this*? You can be *that*. Your life isn't limited to conditional happiness based upon your circumstances.

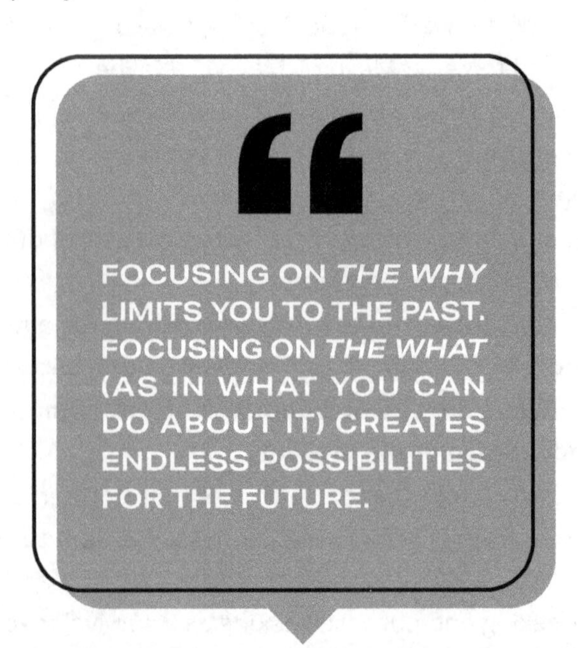

If you're ready to do the work to change your mindset, you will change your life. Ready? Read on.

CONCEPT ONE:

FOCUS ON WHAT YOU *CAN* CONTROL, NOT ON WHAT YOU *CAN'T.*

I was born with a congenital birth defect that gave me a shorter left arm and three missing fingers. Imagine being the only kid in your school with a disability. I'll tell you firsthand (pun intended), it's no fun at all.

My parents said God made me special. They tried hard to protect me, so they enrolled me in a little Christian school where I was in classes with kids I grew up with, who were all familiar with my hand, so my disability was a non-issue. One day, we found out our school was closing, and we were being forced to go elsewhere for middle school. I'd be in a different school than my best friend. I wasn't happy about being separated from him, but I was looking forward to making some new friends. Friends like Crystal—the prettiest girl in my class, and my first real crush.

During the first week of school, I decided I had to talk to this girl. I sat at the back of the classroom and she sat up front, next to the teacher's desk. Before class started one day, I walked right up to her and started a conversation with her. The other kids started laughing, and I didn't understand what was so funny until I looked down and noticed that Crystal was holding a stapler, pretending her hand looked like mine. Then she called me Claw Boy... in front of everyone.

I shoved my hand in my pocket, and I didn't take it out for seven years.

This wasn't an 80-20 rule type of thing. When I say I didn't take my hand out of my pocket, I mean it. If I was out in public, I refused to take my hand out of my pocket. I devised different ways to accomplish tasks with one hand in my pocket. I ran a mile for a PE test with that hand in my pocket. I'd let people punch me when I was in a fight, rather than take my hand out of my pocket. If I forgot to use the one-shoulder method with my backpack before I left the house, when I got to school, I'd go to the bathroom to take my backpack off.

Once, on a field trip to the Washington Monument, security guards asked me to remove my hand from my pocket. I refused. (I almost got arrested for that.) With all my classmates looking on, I was surrounded and forced to show my hand. It was humiliating. On that same trip, I had to share a room, so I kept my hand in my pocket while I slept. The kids actually made up a song about me: "The hand in the pocket kid." (It wasn't very original.)

Nobody ever challenged me and said, "Bro, don't hide your hand. Screw that." While that wasn't anyone else's responsibility, I wish someone had found the courage to challenge me. My parents didn't know I was hurting so much. I never told them or my teachers what was happening to me. I was too embarrassed. I didn't want my parents to have to deal with having a kid who was being bullied. They had enough to deal with, having a kid with a disability.

I didn't cope with my struggles in a productive way back then. I don't think any kid copes with their struggles in a productive way, but, as adults, it's our responsibility to learn how to cope with those things. Back then, I was focusing on what I could not control (other people's reactions) instead of what I could control (my response). I was giving myself lemons... and I drank that self-deprecating lemon juice for almost seventeen years (until I figured out how to sweeten my mindset).

Hiding my hand was easier than dealing with things. I should have spoken up. I should have talked to my parents... my teachers... anyone who could have helped make the situation better. But kids don't usually have the maturity to understand the difference between reacting and responding. Hell, many adults don't fully understand the difference between the two. I didn't understand the difference myself until much later in life.

So, what is the difference between reacting and responding?

When a person *reacts* to a situation, it's based on immediate emotion. The in-the-moment, knee-jerk reaction. Sticking my hand in my pocket was reacting.

When a person *responds* to a situation, it's based on a more mindful and carefully thought-out process, still influenced by emotion, but not dictated by it. Talking to someone about what I was going through would have been responding.

Say you're being bullied at work. You have the choice to either let the bully control you and believe what they're saying (react) or you report the incident, admit it's not your fault, and go up the chain of command until it's taken seriously (respond). If the person bullying you is at the top of that chain of command, you still have options. You can get a new job or report the issue to authorities. There's always an option. There's always a choice. There's always *something* you can control, to better the situation.

Oh, but Chris, you don't understand. I can't get a new job. I live in a small town and my elderly parents are here, so I can't move, and there's nothing else for me.

Look, I get it. There might be challenges. And by *might*, I mean there definitely always are challenges. I never said this would be easy. But that doesn't make my statement less true. There is *always* an option. There's *always* a choice. There's always *something* you can do to better the situation. Even if you live in a place where there actually are no other jobs at all. You could retrain. Become your own boss. You could decide that the daily commute to where there are jobs outweighs the misery that is staying where you are now. You could convince your elderly parents to move with you. See where I'm going here?

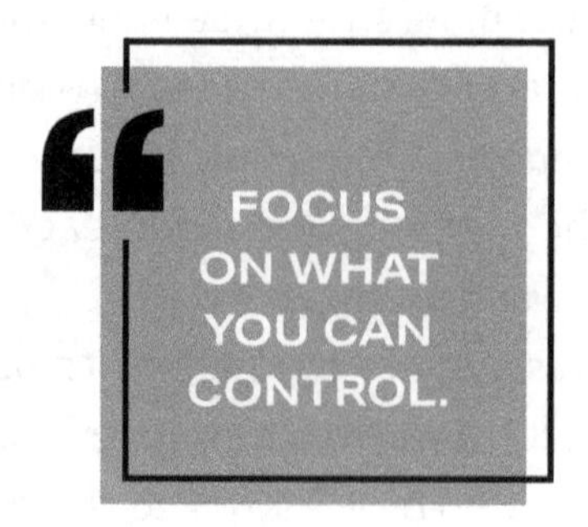

Don't just let it go. Don't sit down and accept something that is not pleasant, if you have the ability to control it. Don't accept a label just because someone puts one on you. Don't be afraid to get up and leave a toxic environment.

Some people drag themselves out of bed at 7am every day to go to a job they despise. You might do this yourself. (I know

I did.) Day after day, month after month, sometimes for years and years. You have yourself convinced that you do this because you have no choice. But that's bullshit. It's not true. You have a choice. You're just stuck in a comfy negative routine.

People enjoy a routine of hard. They get comfortable in discomfort. Especially when that discomfort becomes routine.

But you don't have to be comfortable in hardship. I mean, waking up everyday at 7am to face a job that makes you miserable is already hard... so why should changing it be viewed as any harder?

> "I learned many great lessons from my father, not the least of which was that you can fail at what you don't want so you might as well take a chance on doing what you love." — Jim Carrey

You have options. If you really believe you have no way out, then you still have one choice left. **You can change the way you think** about that job. A tiny conscious shift from "this job sucks" to "this job allows me to pay rent" will help. You could choose to focus on finding one friendly face at work to make the days more tolerable. You could ask for more responsibilities to maybe liven things up. The way you think about your situation is something you always have 100% control over. Nobody can take that away from you.

> "That's all the freedom we can hope for—the freedom to choose our prison." — Lucy Maud Montgomery

Focusing on what you can't control is like trying to determine the outcome of a movie you did not direct or write.

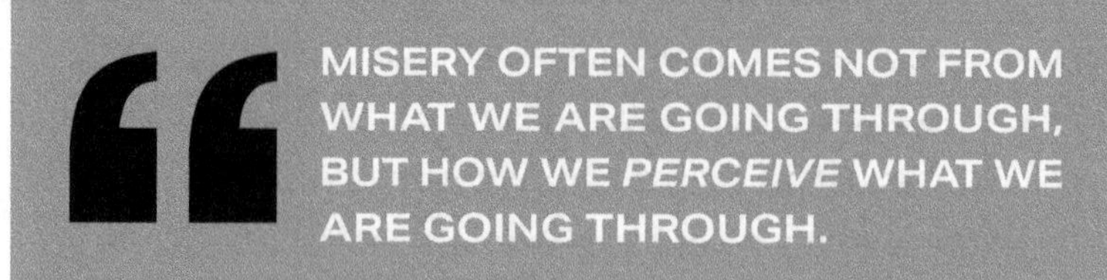

Stop creating the lemons if you don't want them.

Lemons are delicious in pie or lemonade, but would you squirt lemon juice in your chocolate milk? (Ew.) Not all life's recipes call for lemons. If you create lemons in your life, be sure to use them wisely.

You are not powerless. As long as it doesn't pose a threat to your safety[1], you can remove yourself from most situations. You can't control what other people do to you, but you can control how you react. **We have a lot of power in what we can do, but we render ourselves powerless by the way we think.** We remove the control that we do have in most, if not all, scenarios, simply by reacting rather than responding.

In my case, I was born with a disability. I also have Type 1 Diabetes. Those are facts. I could view them as negatives and be consumed about the whys, but that does nothing for me. Zero. Worrying about the whys is focusing on things I can't control.

I refuse to be angry or sad or upset for the rest of my life over something that will never change. I could keep asking why and looking for someone to blame. But what would that do? I can't change anything. I can't control the future. I can only control my reaction right now. I can't magically change my hand. I can't blame away my diabetes. It's a waste of time to think like that. And it also depletes my ability to ever become something more than my conditions.

> THE QUALITY OF YOUR LIFE DEPENDS ON THE QUALITY OF YOUR THOUGHTS. YOU MAY NOT BE ABLE TO GAIN THE UPPER HAND OVER OUTSIDE CIRCUMSTANCES, BUT YOU CAN ALWAYS GAIN THE UPPER HAND OVER YOURSELF.

Why do we continue to get so stuck in our own downward spiral? Why do we convince ourselves that we have to keep getting up at 7am for a job we hate, as if that's our only choice? Do we glorify negativity and hardship? I believe we do.

> WHEN YOUR PERSPECTIVE OF *WHAT IS* GETS PITTED AGAINST YOUR PERSPECTIVE OF *WHAT SHOULD BE*, IT WILL BE IMPOSSIBLE TO LIVE A GOOD LIFE.

Why do we feel the need to convince ourselves that our life is not good enough?

There's an old story about two children who were best friends: one was poor and one was rich. The poor family invited the rich family over for a meal. While the kids were having fun playing and the hosts lovingly prepared a meal for everyone to share, the rich parents were appalled at the rough state of the house.

When the wealthy family went home, the parents said to their child, "you are lucky that we have so much more than they do. Did you see how they live?"

"Yes," the boy said, "I saw that they are happy and love each other and don't need anything else to enjoy life. I hope that we can be poor someday."

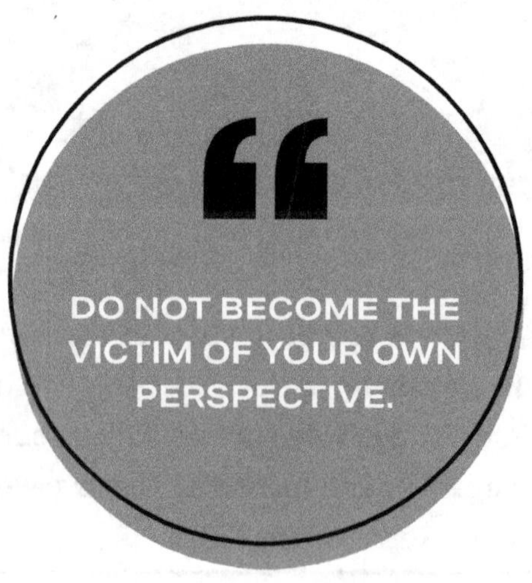

Don't get caught up in the story you're telling yourself, of what you don't have.

Whatever you project, you get good at. People practise negativity. It is easy and natural in our brains. Our society engages in a "who has it worse" culture of competition that makes no sense. Who worked more hours? Who got the least amount of sleep? Who has more bills? Do you really want to win that competition? There are no hardship awards in life. Nobody is going to say, "Hey, you're having the crappiest time. Here's a medal!" Life does not work that way.

It's easier to drag ourselves to that crappy job than it is to face change. But why?

You're putting yourself in a losing position because it's safe. It comforts you. Even though it makes you miserable, staying in a negative cycle takes less energy than trying to enact change. The first step toward change is often the hardest but the most vital to breaking that negative cycle. There's a strange clarity in calamity.

Sure, there might be a freeing feeling when you accept that life is shit, even though in the back of your mind, you know you could probably do something about it. But even though that misery sometimes feels paralyzing, that's when you need to make the move. To paraphrase Isaac Newton, an object in motion stays in motion and an object at rest stays at rest. When you have an object at rest, it is damn hard to change direction.

When a car dies in the middle of the road, the first few pushes are really difficult, but once it starts rolling, it's easier to push. Now, if that car is on an incline and it's rolling back on you, you have a choice. You can stop pushing and let it run you over. Or you can root your feet, acknowledge it might take energy to get momentum, and trust that putting the effort in the right direction will pay off.

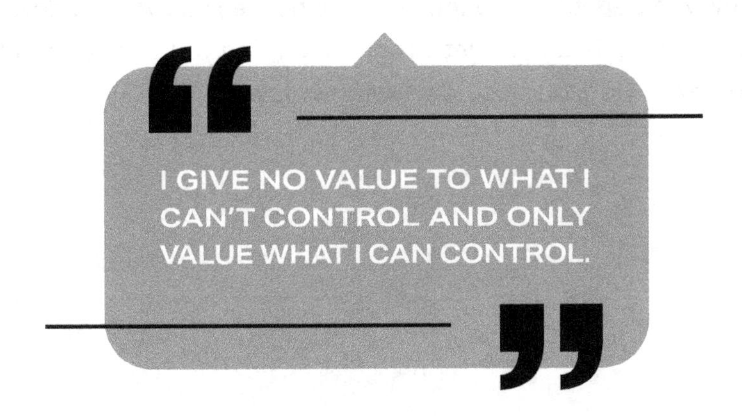

I cannot control how anyone acts when they see my hand. But I can control how I handle their reactions to me.

I used to take everyone's reactions personally. Not because of what they thought of me but because of what *I* thought of me. But now that I have the upper hand over my responses and my perspectives, I'm secure in knowing that regardless of how they feel about me, I'm not broken or freaky or weird. I'm a badass dude with a cool ass arm.

You get to decide on every single move you make through this game of life. You are in control of your next move—your next decision—even if it's just the way you choose to think about it.

Stressing about what you cannot control will not change the situation. So, the next time you face a sucky thing, ask yourself, *what can I do to make this suck less?*

Let's say you lose your job or decide to quit. Your employment status does not dictate your worth, but you have bills to pay so let's figure this out. What can you do with where you are right now that will put you in a position to succeed, if not immediately then in the near future?

Can you update your resume? Can you apply to jobs? Can you reach out to friends for recommendations for jobs? Can you drive for Uber or Lyft? Can you buy things at a yard sale and sell them on Craigslist or Facebook Marketplace? (Google the guy who traded a red paperclip for a house.) Can you cut down on spending? Can you get a roommate? Can you do any sort of freelance work on a site like Fiverr or Upwork?

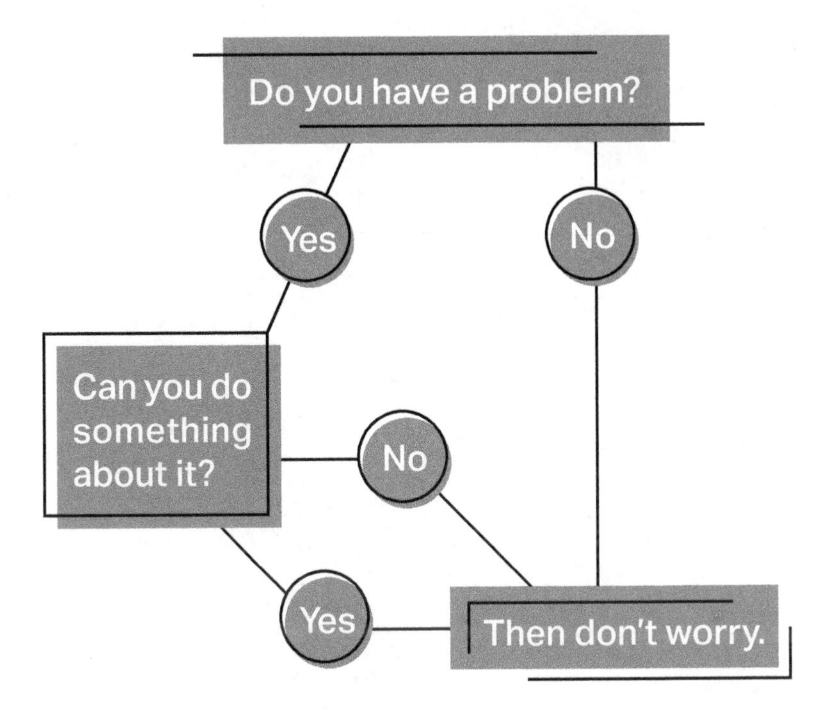

As Tony Robbins says, the biggest resource you have is being resourceful. But you don't need to be Tony Robbins to realize that your power to succeed lies in your power to problem solve—first, in your head, and then in a tangible way. If you fall into quicksand, that sucks. It's random and you can't control it. But, you aren't going to just shrug your shoulders and let yourself sink, are you? No. You're going to reach for a branch, yell for help, try something (anything!) to get yourself out of that scenario.

Is there something happening in your life that you aren't happy about? Focus on what you can control. Not on what you can't. That's going to give you the upper hand. Every single time.

[1] *I fully recognize that in some situations, you may put yourself at risk by taking direct action. Domestic abuse, gun violence, racially based attacks, and sexual assaults come to mind. In these cases, please do whatever you need to do to minimize harm. While there is help out there, I do recognize that these situations warrant a different change of approach than other daily struggles.

CONCEPT TWO:

WE BUILD OUR OWN CAGES TO BE LESS "YOU ARE SHIT" AND MORE "WE ARE SHIT."

A grown elephant can weigh anywhere between 4,000 and 14,000 pounds. In order to get the upper hand over an animal this large, a common (horrible, yet effective) method of "training" elephants is to tie them to a chair or a stake in the ground when they're babies.

An elephant can easily move a stake or a chair—they're massive animals. But they grow up believing they're helpless as long as there's a rope tied to their leg. When that baby elephant has grown into a giant animal with the physical ability to crush a human, all someone has to do to maintain control over them is tie a rope to their leg, and they won't even bother to struggle.

Just because you couldn't do something yesterday doesn't mean you can't do it today. Take every opportunity for change toward the life that you want.

This story is an example of learned helplessness. The elephant knows they can't move. They're not upset that they can't move because that's just life. The elephant is confident in the fact that they can't move when there's a rope around their foot. The elephant accepts their learned helplessness, and that's how many people live.

Learned helplessness is a condition where people suffer from a sense of powerlessness, usually felt because of a traumatic event or persistent failure to succeed. It's also thought to be one of the underlying causes for depression.

Basically, learned helplessness is when you stop trying. Learned helplessness is when you create a cage for yourself as a protective mechanism to prevent future failings.

I've been there. I felt that and lived it for so long. Have you ever seen those old movies where there's a guy in a jail cell screaming to get out, and the camera pans out and the door is open? It's funny when we see it on TV, until we realize we're doing the exact same thing in our own lives—we wrote a script putting ourselves in a make-believe cage with every opportunity to get out but no desire to leave.

We find ourselves imprisoned in a cage we built with a lock we have the key to, and, vocally, we want to get out, but, realistically, we're more comfortable inside that cage. We pretend to want to break out of the cage so much, but, in reality, the cage isn't holding us back—it's keeping us safe. Safe from potential failing. Safe from the outside world, safe from unexplored possibilities. It could be good or it could be bad, but it's damage control.

Caged animals become conditioned to believe a situation is unchangeable. "Conditioned to believe" and reality are different.

We're conditioned as kids and adults to believe that we all have a "cage" (a lifestyle we live within). The world is massive, but our world is small. You go to the same store, do the same things—your cage is the lifestyle you set for yourself. But I want to remove the negative connotation of the cage because it's kind of epic.

Our house is a form of a cage that we feel comfortable in. Dogs are crated in a cage that becomes their comfort zone. Cages are seen as a bad thing because people think it's inescapable, but how can you escape something you built and have access to 24/7? That's a matter of decision.

There is a difference between being imprisoned against your will and being in a cage that you built. The elephant may weigh 14,000 pounds, but something tells me they didn't physically build the cage. The elephant lacks dexterity to hammer a nail. The animal is not a general contractor. While caged animals might not be able to escape their prison, people who create their cages can leave at any time, or they may expand the size of their cage. You don't need to get rid of your cage; you just have to know it doesn't confine your ability to live your life.

Your cage can be a comfort zone—that's not a bad thing—but you have to be willing to leave the cage and come back. I don't like when people create fake parameters for themselves and then get mad when they live within those parameters. People give themselves parameters like, "Because of my past, I'll never be happy or succeed or break this habit."

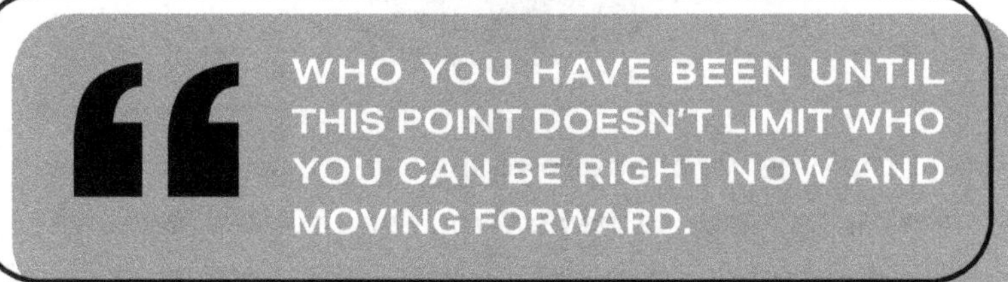

You made a cage that isn't real, and you're upset when life is going on outside that imaginary cage you built yourself.

"It's just who I am" = cage
"It's how I always deal with problems" = cage
"It's how I've always been" = cage
"I'll never be able to be like that person on social media" = cage

It's those thoughts or limiting beliefs that are cages around your potential. You're creating a cage around the lifestyle that you want. Even though you made those cages that came with those locks, you feel like you don't have the key. That's another lie we tell ourselves.

Animals in cages have been imprisoned. When the opportunity arises to escape, an animal will make a run for it. But humans, even when the opportunity arises, do not leave their self-imposed cages. That is the problem with learned helplessness.

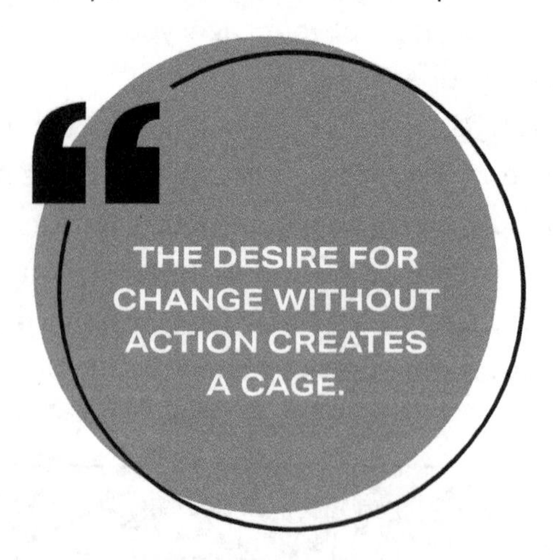

From the time we are quite young, we are taught things we can and can't do and see the powerful effect societal stereotypes have on developing preset parameters without our input...

- Being a professional athlete is nearly impossible.
- Most people never make it through med school.
- Being an actor or singer or artist is not a real job.
- Small town people only have small town lives.
- Your race/gender/religion/disability will limit your success level.
- You have to continue the family business.
- You can't have donuts for breakfast. (That's a damn lie. I've had donuts at the Hilton's continental breakfast, thank you very much.)

I'm sure you're familiar with all of these statements, and I hope that you recognize all of them are cages built around your potential that you do not have to accept or stay in.

Imagine if The Rock believed wrestling wasn't a real career. Imagine if Barack Obama believed there could never be a Black president of the United States. Imagine if Stephen King believed that there's no money in writing books. Imagine if the doctor who saved your loved one's life believed they could never make it through med school.

A cage can be built for us as a place for protection, or it can be built as a form of self sabotage. There are many reasons we build cages. A cage may be different for you than for me. For me, my cage was like being under house arrest. I was allowed to live my life, but my cage was my glove covering my disability.

Animals in captivity find themselves in enclosed habitats. Criminals find themselves in prisons. Even during a natural disaster or under severe conditions, we might find ourselves stuck in our homes for days or weeks on end. Containment from external forces outside of our control, for the most part, is different than the cages we build for ourselves inside our minds. While we can't always control imprisonment, we can control the cages that we build for ourselves. We are not confined by walls that we can deconstruct. That's the difference. No, you can't deconstruct your cerebral palsy or your diabetes or any of the things that you can't control. But what can you control? Your outlook on life.

Anyone struggling with a difference or discrimination or any sort of adversity that they cannot fix, control, or change, **who has changed their perspective, has changed the cage they found themselves in.** We don't have to be positive all the time—just understand what you can control, and that there's no point in focusing on what you can't.

We need to take our learned helplessness and apply it to an abled present. Even if you're physically disabled like I am, you have the ability to be present and create different actions and habits to turn past failings into future successes. If you built a cage around yourself because of a learned helplessness trait, that's okay. Just make sure the cage you built also has a door.

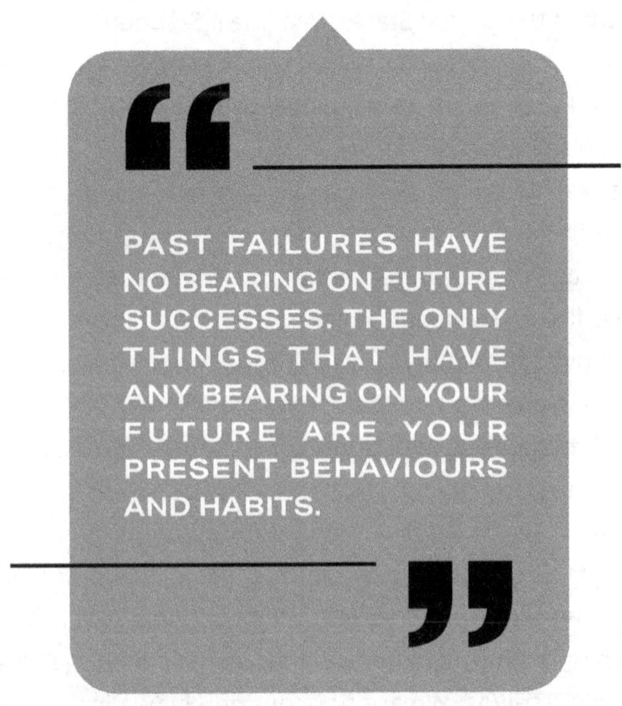

A few years ago, I was at the gym lifting weights with an adaptive device to compensate for my shorter arm. A woman approached me and asked if I'd be interested in working with her eleven-year- old son, David, who has cerebral palsy. She said, "He can't walk or talk very well, but he has a great attitude."

I started working with David at their home on the weekends, and I quickly fell in love with the kid. David was truly happy. He didn't care when he messed up. He was completely unfazed by how he looked or by his physical limitations. His attitude lifted my spirits, and it made me feel good just to be around him.

One day, David told me some kids at school were making fun of him. My first reaction was that I wanted to hunt down these children and dropkick them in the throat. But David shrugged it off. "Cerebral palsy doesn't define me," he said. And he went back to working on his exercises.

I was floored. The thought processes that this kid had established at the age of eleven were the kind that some adults never learn. And, to be honest, it took me over seventeen years to figure them out for myself.

David wouldn't let cerebral palsy define him, and, therefore, it didn't limit him. Six months after we started working together, he ran on the beach for the first time.

I didn't cure David's cerebral palsy. And I didn't fix his mindset. He fixed mine. The reality is, David will have cerebral palsy for the rest of his life, but what he won't have is a cage of learned helplessness preventing him from attempting and reaching the untapped potential that I know he has.

That kid taught me more about myself and my condition than anyone else ever has. Back then, I was still hiding my hand with a glove, as I had been for years. I was ashamed of who I made myself out to be because of my disability. I was so confident that I would never show my hand, I had no fear about it. Just like how I used to be afraid of roller coasters, but I'm not anymore because I know I'll never go on one. **I'm not afraid of something I know will never happen.** I was totally confident in my insecurity.

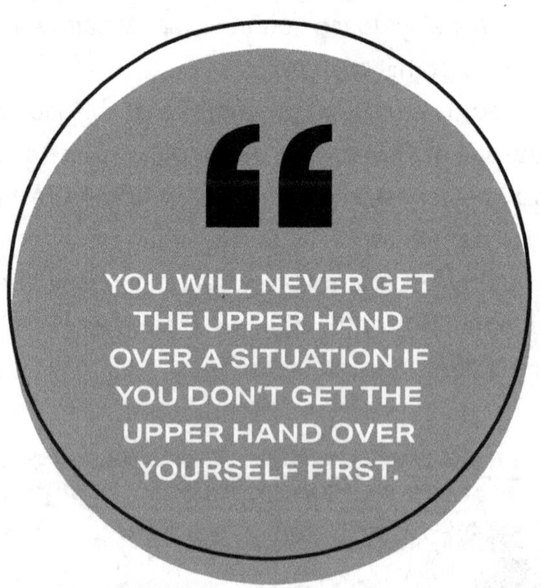

Think about a moment when you had a negative thought about yourself. A time where you caught yourself thinking a losing thought. *I'm not worth it... I suck... I'll never get a better job than this...* Got one? Okay. Hold it for a minute.

When I was younger, I battled losing thoughts all day, every day. When I woke up in the morning, my first thought was a losing one. *How will I hide my hand today?*

There is a lot of noise in our heads, and that's okay. Your job is to determine which of your thoughts will help you and which will hurt you. This takes work, and it is an ongoing process, but it is possible to do. When I need help sorting out the noise, I use the Catch–Challenge–Change concept.

1. Catch the negative thought
2. Challenge the thought with reality
3. Change it to actively improve your mental health

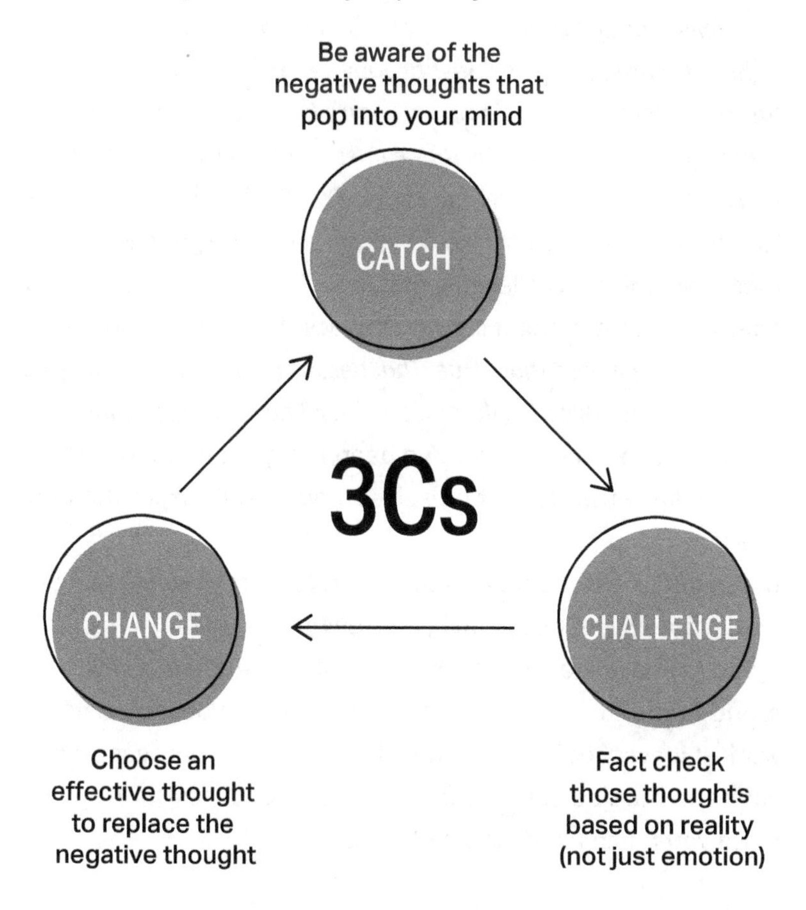

When I catch myself having a negative thought about showing my hand, I **challenge** it. *Hey, Chris, does anybody at the store actually give a shit that your hand is different? Is anybody here going to care enough about my hand to pay for my stuff or my bills?* The answer is no. So, screw that. I **change** that thought. My hand is different. I can't change that. But nobody looking at my hand in a store is going to take away the value I have as a person.

Go back to that negative thought I asked you to hold onto a second ago. I'll use the common *I'm not worth it* as an example.

You **catch** that thought, which is maybe the toughest part of this because awareness requires honesty.

After you catch it, you **challenge** it. *Am I really not worth it or am I telling myself that because of a bad moment I'm experiencing right now? Am I using my past negative experiences to predict my future success? Am I deciding my future based on my past? Is that something I have to do or is that something I am choosing to do? If I had a flat tire, would I set the car on fire?* Probably not. Because turning a small problem into a big one is never a good idea. And there's no point in challenging that thought unless you're going to **change** it. What thought can you replace that negative one with? *I've failed in the past, that's true. That doesn't mean I'll keep failing, as long as I change this thought process. I don't have to become my past.*

Some people feel like they've been assigned a role based on the narrative they feed themselves, and they think it's the only role they can play for the rest of their lives. But in your life, you're the writer, the director, and the actor. Is this the role you want to play forever? If not... catch, challenge, change.

Catch–Challenge–Change is like brushing your teeth. If you do it once a month, it's not going to do much for you. You have to work at it every day. All the time. If you only use a gas gage when you're on the side of the road completely out of gas, it isn't going to do you much good. Same idea here.

The goal isn't to be positive all the time. The goal is to win each moment of the day, and that comes from being actively present in the way you think. If you fail to do that, you're going to be on autopilot and emotionally reacting to all of those bad thoughts. How can you deal with a problem if you're not present?

I think people take lessons from past experiences and create behaviours that guarantee their failure.

What happens is that they end up with a self-deprecating narrative, and because of the narrative that **they** themselves started, they start behaving in a way that predicts their failure.

A new failure happens, and they say, *See? I was right. I failed and I will always be a failure*. This connects past failure to future failure, and what is missing is present ability and present choices. **If you act in a way that predicts your failure, you can't be upset when you fail.** When you start building that cage around yourself—when you create your own limits or walls, not around what you can't control but around what you can control, you can't be upset. You can move the walls! You can act differently. **You have to learn to do something different if you want something different.** Every time you date a toxic person, you get hurt. Again and again. You have a right to the pain but not a right to be upset about the pain.

Just because you have a bad thought doesn't mean you have to live your bad thoughts.

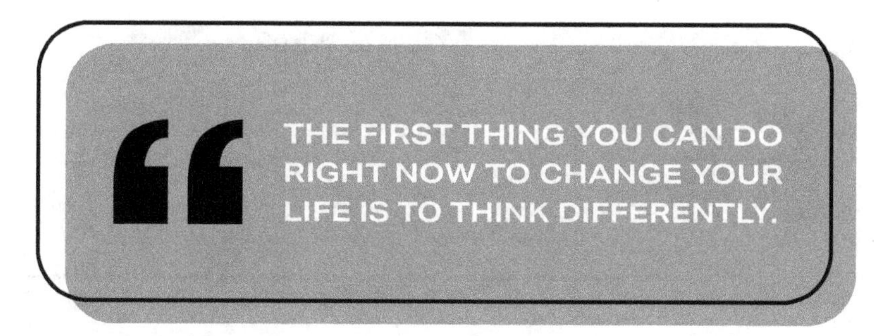

Life doesn't happen in the extremes. You navigate life in the middle, so you're not always slamming on the brakes; you're just driving. The bad shit happens when you're not aware or paying attention—when you let bad behaviours sneak in and leave you on autopilot. Stop living on autopilot.

Challenge every thought that predicts your own unhappiness. Those thoughts are not coming from anyone else. The only way you will ever have the upper hand over yourself is if you have the upper hand over your thoughts. Ask yourself, *Am I doing something that's causing me to fail? Am I doing something that's causing me to bring this negative belief about myself to light?* Usually the answer is yes.

Sometimes, for example, people want to look better, but they aren't willing to change their actions and habits so they can have that body they desire. Most people want a better life without changing their habits, thoughts, and/or behaviours. But you can't have one without the other. That's not how life works. Everyone wants to hang out at the finish line without running the race.

People want the goal and not to put in the time or work to get it. Reframe your perspective on goals to see habits as requirements that make up goals.

I hate goal setting, and I honestly never get anything from it, unless there's a clear commitment to action that I start immediately. Goals without action behind them are not really goals at all.

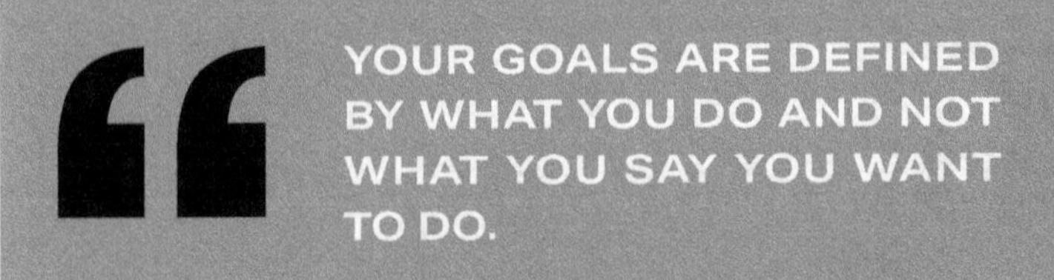

Tons of people say you have to write down your goals. That's not enough! Pretend your goal is to run a marathon. Great. You don't practise hanging out by the finish line. You practise by running. By idolizing the finish line, we don't think about the steps needed to achieve that goal. Your goal shouldn't be to run a marathon. It should be going to the gym six days a week and running five miles a day.

The goal should not be to attend a body builder show. It should be hitting the gym every day and prepping meals consistently.

The goal should be the work, not the end game.

People see goals as a finite thing, not as habits. But they should be seen as habits. This makes your goals more achievable. Goals look nice on paper, but there is a disconnect with the work required to reach them. Goal setting is like taking drugs. People love it, and it makes them feel good. You write your goals down on paper and think, *oh look at how close I am to my goals!* No. You did nothing. You wrote them down. Now what?

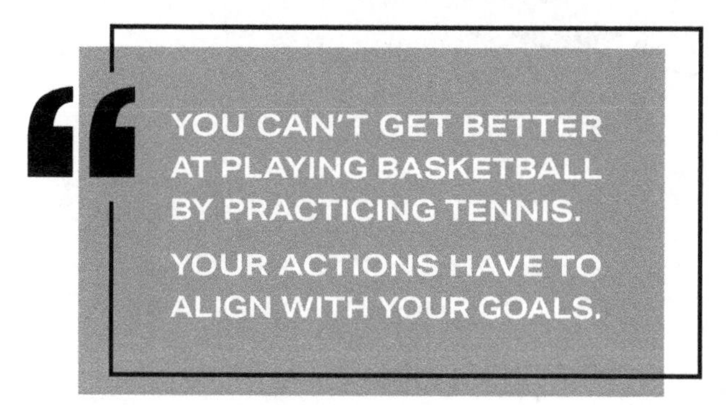

Truthfully, what you're struggling with is not uncommon, and you're not alone. The concept of struggle is ancient. Many other people have fought the same battle and some are doing it with a different perspective that might help you. **Fortunately, the cage that holds your limiting beliefs isn't locked, and you can walk out at any time.**

CONCEPT THREE:

STOP TOUCHING THE HOT STOVE

When you put your hand on a hot stove once, you get burned and learn that if you put your hand on the stove, it hurts, so you don't want to do that anymore.

Mentally, we get burned by the fire over and over and almost come to love that feeling of controlled pain. We fear the uncertainty of life so much so that we're willing to predictably hurt ourselves to avoid the unknown.

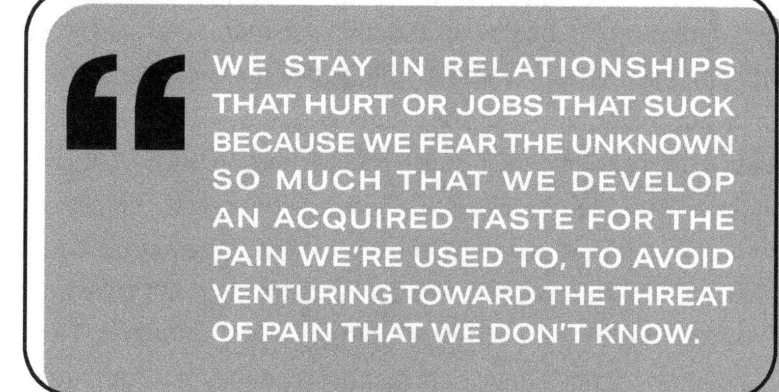

There's so much comfort in certainty that even if you know something's not going to be good, it's better and more comforting than not knowing at all, especially to an anxious mind. We are creating a pattern that we become stuck in, and we are all stuck in patterns, regardless of where we are in life.

People who repeat good societal patterns once learned the value of doing the right thing and following the rules. They put their seatbelt on, treat people a certain way, and use their manners. They are in that pattern.

Your pattern is going to determine the amount of trouble you do or don't get into — your pattern of self-talk and your pattern of being able to buffer thoughts that predict your downfall. The pattern of your self-talk will determine how successful you are because it will encourage the behaviours that lead to success. The patterns you reinforce will put you in a position to either get burned or avoid self sabotage. The pattern you choose to allow and reinforce will grow. And to break a bad pattern, it takes acknowledging it and changing it consistently over time. You have to be able to say, I am done touching the stove. Now and forever moving forward.

These patterns are subconscious. We don't always know they're happening. You can be driving and think, oh man, I changed lanes but I don't remember doing it. Things like driving or breathing are so automatic, you just don't think about it. And sometimes a negative thought process is automatic. It's hard to learn from your mistakes if you're not aware of them—especially if you repeat them so much that you don't consider them to be a problem.

People who follow self-destructive patterns don't take into account whether what they're doing is right or wrong. They consider their actions to be right just because they're what they've always done.

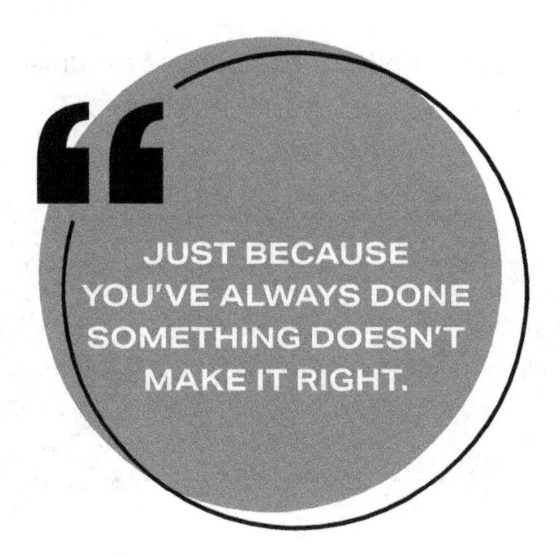

Whether you're someone who dates toxic people who only take from you, engages in illegal activities, or takes jobs that aren't fulfilling... it doesn't matter.

I hid my hand. I continued to tell myself that is what I do... that it was who I was.

But hiding my hand wasn't who I was. It's how I was deciding to be in that moment and what I decided to do in that moment. I acted like I didn't have a choice but to hide my hand. That was a lie that I continually told myself—a self-destructive pattern I was stuck in.

When you self-destruct, you have a chance to choose what you're going to do in that moment. Many times, we are aware of the things we need to do. We have priorities and deadlines and goals and behaviours and thoughts that, if accomplished, will improve our quality of life. Conversely, in not doing them, we choose the behaviours that lead to self-destruction.

We are usually aware of our bad reactions to hardship, yet we still choose the reactions that we know will hurt us more than help us. You have an opportunity to change. I think it comes from small momentary decisions to break a pattern. First, you have to be aware of the pain you're experiencing and what is causing it. If you're constantly deflecting to outside circumstances, you'll never know the cause.

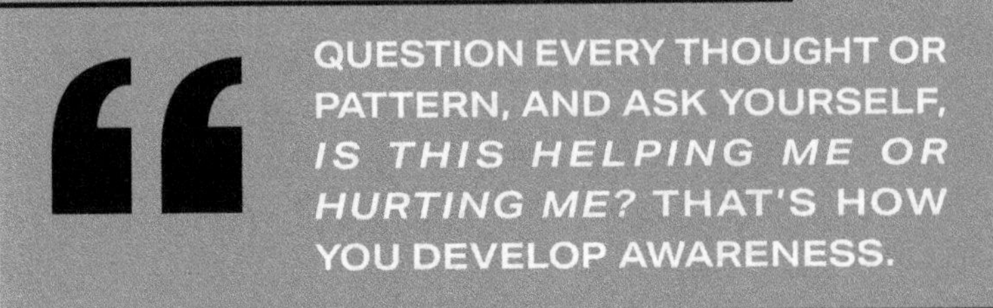

QUESTION EVERY THOUGHT OR PATTERN, AND ASK YOURSELF, *IS THIS HELPING ME OR HURTING ME?* THAT'S HOW YOU DEVELOP AWARENESS.

It's like not extinguishing the fire behind you because you're too busy looking for who started it. Stop looking for the arsonist in the moment, and put out the fire.

We get into these thought patterns, and they just take over after we get so far down a self-destructive path. I guaranteed myself that I was never going to be comfortable with my disability. That was not an option. The second I decided to hide my hand, I was okay with this line of thinking, and I became committed to hiding my disability for the rest of my life. I decided that's who I was. *My name is Chris. I have a disability and I hide my hand*. I made it part of me.

That self-belief **makes you play the game of life to not lose, rather than to win.** And that is truly what I believed of myself and who I was. You'll never get into a car accident if you never leave your house. You'll never lose a basketball game if you don't play. And if you hide your insecurities from yourself, you won't have to face them.

People are so scared of losing what little comfort they have, it can be debilitating. For me, covering my disability with a glove was my comfort. I planned on wearing the glove for the rest of my life and never thought it was debilitating, until one day I couldn't find my glove, and I refused to go to school. I didn't have my comfort. When you're in the position of your comfort being disrupted, you realize your comfort is heavily laced in insecurity and unmanaged problems.

That fear of losing and of being uncomfortable doesn't feel good. Deciding to create a new thought process, unfortunately, doesn't pay off right away, and you will probably fail multiple times. But just because you don't experience a big win the first time you try something, that doesn't mean you get to give up.

Imagine if every athlete gave up the first time they competed and didn't win. We would have no professional sports! But that's how people act with inflexible self-beliefs. They try something once, it doesn't pay off, and they return to what was comfortable... even though what was comfortable was painful. They walk around with a portable stove just so they can burn themselves.

Over 80% of people quit their New Year's resolutions after three weeks, running back to their old habits.

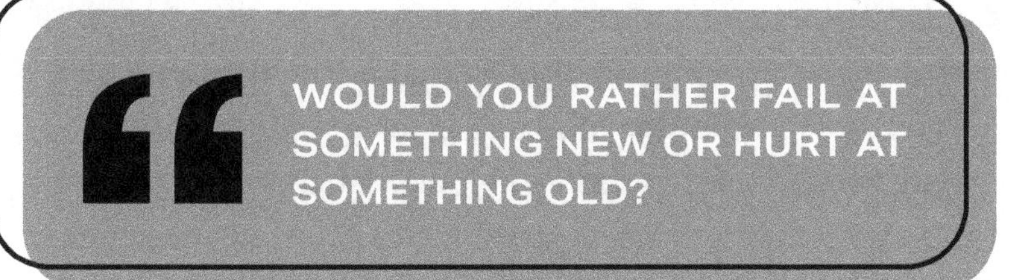

Why are we so comfortable with the pain we give ourselves that we accept it instead of trying to get better? Why do we cling to the thoughts that we think comfort us, when, really, we know they're hurting us?

There's a fear of losing something that is ours, whether it's a thought or a material object. If you have to start clearing out the problems in your life—whether you're a hoarder or a person with harmful thought patterns—you have the responsibility to get rid of the things you at one point told yourself you need. That's hard.

I believe when we try to get past a negative experience, we actually hold onto it to remind ourselves of the lesson. For me? I was holding onto the pain of being bullied. I wanted to use that example to never let people label me again. But while I was trying to teach myself a lesson, I was replaying the classroom teasing event and filling my mind with so many negative thoughts of pain and humiliation that I was harming myself. I didn't need those negative thoughts to take over my life, in order to get the lesson.

Once the lesson is learned, there's no reason to dwell on it. The actual experience serves little to no good once you get the lesson behind it. By removing the negative experiences of bullying and self-hate, I can see that I alone determine my value. And I choose to do so effectively every day moving forward without reliving what hurt me in the past, which, honestly? Would just burden my present and potential future.

You use all the ingredients to make the dish. You don't serve the ingredients. You have to let go of those and focus on what you made as a result. If you order chocolate cake at a restaurant, they don't deconstruct it into flour, sugar, eggs, and whatever the hell else is in cake; they serve you the chocolate cake, and that's what you want—the finished product.

People tend to focus on the negative experiences and not the lessons gained, but they also end up doing this to other people, unknowingly. I see parents lowering their kids' self-esteem all the time, whether they know it or not, by reinforcing negative lessons. Consider the parent who reminds their kid of all the mistakes they've made, over and over.

> "Remember you were so messy, and you left all your stuff on the floor and you tripped and broke your leg? That will teach you not to be messy!"

> "You're so forgetful. Remember when you were supposed to bring in that permission slip and you didn't, so you missed the school trip? You have to stop being forgetful."

How would you feel if you were spoken to this way? Reminding people of every negative experience in their life to teach a lesson isn't constructive. You're putting that negative experience in their face over and over for what? To learn something? At what cost? What long-term effect will your shaming have?

Instead of scolding and harping on the bad things that happened when they were messy, why not focus on the benefits of being less messy to help them improve? Why not offer a solution with the lesson of being forgetful instead of reminding them that they were forgetful before? (Let's be honest, unless you help solve it, they will probably forget this condemnation anyways, too.)

Clarify the lesson, and stop reminding people of the mistake. That goes for you and the people around you.

We don't need to beat ourselves up over every bad thing we've ever done. We did it. It's done. What can we take from it?

Taking your hand off the stove includes forgiving yourself for the bad things, as long as you decide to move forward.

When you are skilled, experienced, and comfortable in your pain, you will cling to it. When challenging that pain as a belief that doesn't serve you, you will immediately try to reframe it as something you don't really need to change. Your pattern is set. Anything that challenges the pain you've tethered yourself to feels so uncomfortable that it's easier to manipulate the evidence than it is to change the belief. I know that first hand.

I was so confident with my disability being a hardship that I had an excuse ready whenever somebody challenged my thoughts. *I have to hide my hand or else people won't like me. I won't be successful. I'll be seen as weak, etc.* Regardless of the evidence I had in knowing I would be happier if I accepted myself, I refused to change my mindset because of the limiting beliefs I had around my differences.

I think everyone today has a contradictory attitude toward messing up. We always give excuses for ourselves, yet we're quick to blame other people. It's so hypocritical and ironic. When we make a mistake, there's always someone to blame, but when someone else makes a mistake, it's their fault... so deep.

> "You're so dumb — stop touching the stove." (Yet, you have your hand on the burner.)
>
> "Yeah, but what you don't understand is..." (There you go again—making excuses for yourself. The thing is, why is your hand on the stove? What will it take to remove it, and how are you going to stop touching it in the future?)

It's easy to make temporary changes. It's Monday, and the diet starts today! It's easier to start the week with a ritual or a quote, but in reality, few people stick to it past Tuesday.

In order to stop these negative patterns, we first have to be mindful of them and recognize our pain.

When we place our hand on the stove, it burns. But when we hold it there, we adapt to the pain. It's much harder to recognize pain that has been ingrained in your culture and your lifestyle. I think the deepest and truest form of pain is the underlying pain that you live with. You know that when you break your arm, it will heal, and you can feel the pain diminishing over time. But you can be slowly breaking your mentality over years and years without that pain ever even registering.

Keeping your hand off the stove means asking yourself constantly:

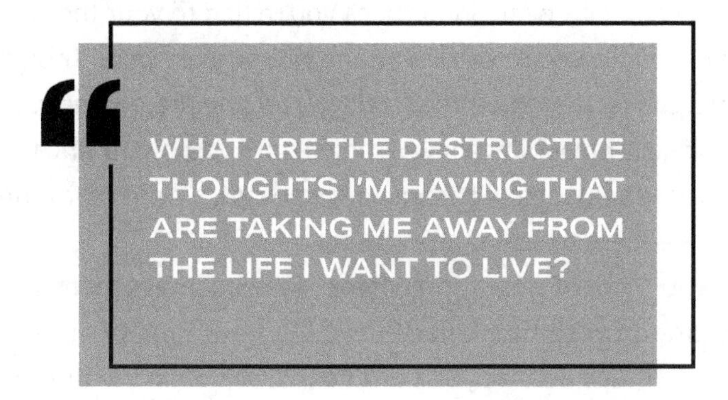

Be real honest with yourself and make it a yes or no. For example, *is the way I think and the life I live, the way I want to end up forever?* (Go back to Catch–Challenge–Change. It will help.)

If the answer is yes, you're good. This isn't a problem. Great.

If the answer is no, you have to keep going and identify what's going on. What are the beliefs, tendencies, and patterns that you're stuck in right now that are making you answer no to that question?

Think about it this way: You're in a room full of friends and you're all making jokes about yourselves. One person says, "Yeah, well I always date people who hate me." When it's your turn to speak, what pattern are you going to say as a joke, but you know it's the truth? In those moments, we are quick to admit our actual flaws. When we say them out loud, though, it feels a little too real. *I drink alone... I never remember to take out the garbage... I don't think I'm going to be successful.* It can be anything.

We learn to live with these things that we tell ourselves. By **living with them** too long, we **live for them**, and that's when life goes a little sideways.

It all goes back to learned helplessness. Not always are you tied to a chair or a post. Sometimes you're tied to your thoughts, and you believe you're stuck with the way you are now. Thought patterns can be reprogrammed, but you are the programmer. You have to figure out what's going wrong before you can fix anything.

History repeats itself because people don't learn from their mistakes—from touching the hot stove.

Can you think of a location where every business that's been established there has failed? It's switched hands countless times... so much so that you can't keep track of all the different businesses it's been. It might be boarded up right now, or maybe it just switched from being a bakery to a tattoo parlour, from a restaurant to a shoe store. You've seen it open and close multiple times, and you wonder why people keep doing this—this location never succeeds.

Isn't it ridiculous to invest so much in something you've seen fail over and over again? You would never do that... right? So why do you invest so much in the negative thought pattern that you know fails over and over? You're quick to judge someone who invests in a location you know will fail but slow to hold yourself accountable for investing in negative thought patterns you know will fail.

Believing and investing in a negative thought pattern is no different than constantly investing in a bad real estate location. You're paying rent toward something that has proven to repeatedly fail. Because you're so stubborn and inflexible in your patterns and beliefs that are crumbling, you still try to make it work.

It's like putting a stick through your own bike spokes, only to get upset and look for someone to blame when you crash. If only there was a mirror nearby to show you who is responsible.

Let's dig a bit more into this...

- What are you currently doing (or not doing) that makes you think less of yourself?
- What are your worst behaviours that are slowing your growth?
- What are your biggest fears, related to your goals? (Hint: these are usually tied to your worst habits)
- How do your bad habits inflame your fears? How are the habits making those fears worse?
- What can you do every day to help combat bad habits or traits?

Remember: setting small goals will set you up for large successes. If you tell yourself you only have to floss one tooth, you'll go to the sink, open the floss, and chances are you'll floss all your teeth. If you tell yourself to just go to the gym and do two push-ups, you'll probably decide to do more once you arrive. You just have to create momentum. The hardest part is starting.

Try the NLP (neuro linguistic programming) technique of changing your phrasing around habits from the present tense ("I always mess everything up") to past tense ("I may have messed up in the past, but I'm not my past patterns and will improve daily").

By reframing the person you are—from being defined by habits of your past to who you used to be—, you can isolate bad habits or patterns to the past. This gives you a chance to think and act differently. By applying a habit of your past to your current self, you are setting up your current and future self to simply become a carbon copy of the past, dictating that how you've "always been" is how you will always be—that's a choice.

Check out this mantra:

Just because of [BAD EVENT] doesn't mean I can't [GOAL] as long as I stop [BAD HABIT] and start [IMPROVE HABIT].

Example:

Just because **I was born with a disability** doesn't mean I can't **be confident in my body** as long as I stop **telling myself I'm broken** and start **embracing who I am**.

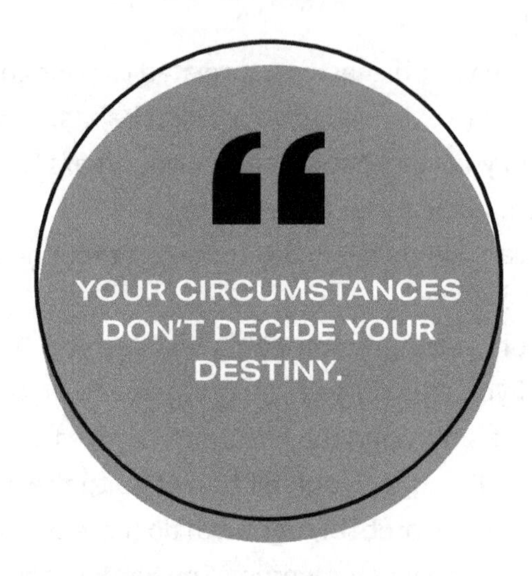

Gaining the upper hand over your patterns gives you the upper hand over your problems. Take your hand off the damn stove.

CONCEPT FOUR:

HARDSHIP ISN'T THE END OF THE WORLD

At one point in his life, Eric Thomas was so down on his luck, he lived in an abandoned property and ate out of trash cans. Feeling very low, Eric spoke with a pastor who helped him to see that his voice was a gift—people tended to listen to him—and he should do something with that gift. Eric took the pastor's advice to heart and developed his skill for speaking.

Today, Eric Thomas is one of the most influential speakers in the world, in terms of reach and performance. To go from being someone who was broke, at rock bottom, and eating out of trash cans, to coming out on top? That kind of success story doesn't happen by chance.

> HARDSHIP DOESN'T GUARANTEE SUCCESS, AND IT DOESN'T GUARANTEE FAILURE.
>
> WHEN YOU MIX IN CHOICE, HARDSHIP CAN BE EITHER THE FUEL THAT PUSHES YOU FORWARD OR THE PLACE WHERE YOUR STORY ENDS.

Nobody knows their true strength if their strength hasn't been tested. You can't say you're the strongest person in powerlifting if you've never lifted weights. You can't say you're the best quarterback if you've never played football. How do you know?

Untested strength is like Monopoly money... you can't use it. That also applies to mental strength. There will undoubtedly be hardship in your life that will require you to use mental strength. **Adversity is a universal language.** That adversity becomes a test that, rather than pass or fail, is strength building or strength depleting.

Your mental strength will be tested, and that is a test you might not always pass. I've had dreams shattered when, at the time, it seemed like my whole world was wrapped up in them. Those events are a test of mental strength.

I don't believe that winners never quit. I believe winners know when to quit. I fought to get into the military, knowing how hard it would be with a disability. I finally got through all of the hoops, but was then diagnosed with Type 1 Diabetes. That is a losing battle. You can't get into the military with Type 1 Diabetes. I could have kept fighting, but I had to know when to switch lanes. I quit because I knew there was nothing I could do to change national policy. I've lost money in business endeavours I knew wouldn't work out. I've lost relationships that I thought were guaranteed. I believe winners know when to change lanes, and that's when new worlds start to open up.

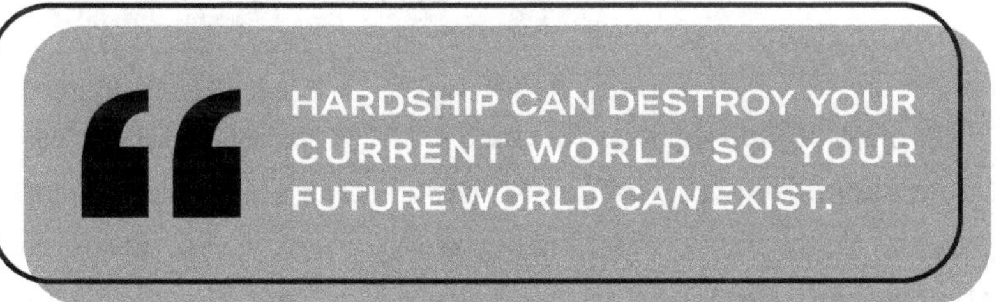

Hardship happens to everyone. I'm not special because I have diabetes or because I'm disabled. Many people experience the same things. But not everyone experiences these things with my perspective. It's my perspective that gives me the upper hand. And your perspective can give *you* the upper hand.

If you know you don't have a fighting chance with the hardship you're facing, cool. You get to give up. You get a pass.

But if you have *any* glimmer of hope, you do not have the right to let hardship be the end for you.

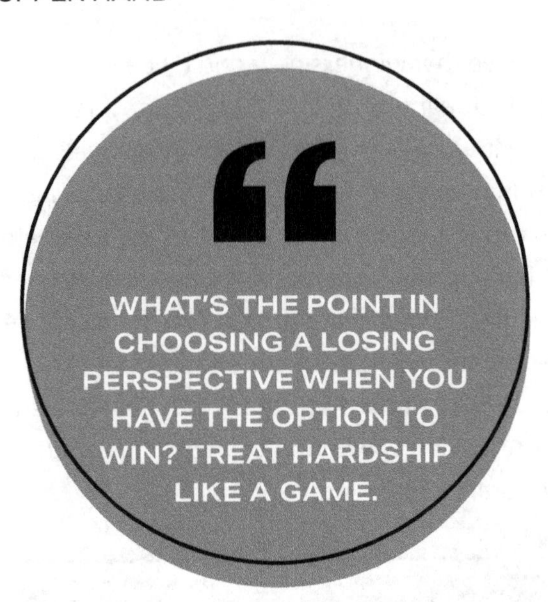

People play video games for the thrill of overcoming obstacles. Some people even pay money to sign up for obstacle courses, so they can go through something absolutely gruelling that has been **strategically designed** to break them. They get muddied and bruised and scraped and fall and punished for not completing the obstacles as intended. And they still smile for the picture at the end and maybe even sign up for another one.

Some people sign up to do escape rooms, where they pay to be locked in a damn room for an hour trying to find their way out. They invest all of their mental energy into looking for clues to find a way out of this scenario. No texting or social media or Netflix—just full focus on solving the problem at hand, at gaining the upper hand over this situation. We have to be just as eager to solve the mystery of the room as we are to finding solutions to our problems.

But, when it comes to our own problems, we do not give it our all. We spend the majority of our time wasting time wherever we choose to waste it, and then complain that we tried everything.

Why will people pay to go through hardship when they think it's going to be fun (choosing that perspective) but when they actually go through struggle they didn't pay for, they complain about it (also choosing that perspective)?

I'm not saying you should look at your hardships as fun, but, if you imagine hardship is a game, it might help you to shift perspective. The obstacle itself might not be fun (it likely isn't), but what *is* fun is looking back and knowing that you conquered it. I can look back and say when I was diagnosed with diabetes, I thought of it as what it is: an incurable autoimmune disease I will have for the rest of my life. For me to conquer that obstacle, I had to let go of what I couldn't control (the disease itself and curing it) and focus on what I could control (managing it and not letting it manage my life). And, in that way, I conquered an unconquerable condition.

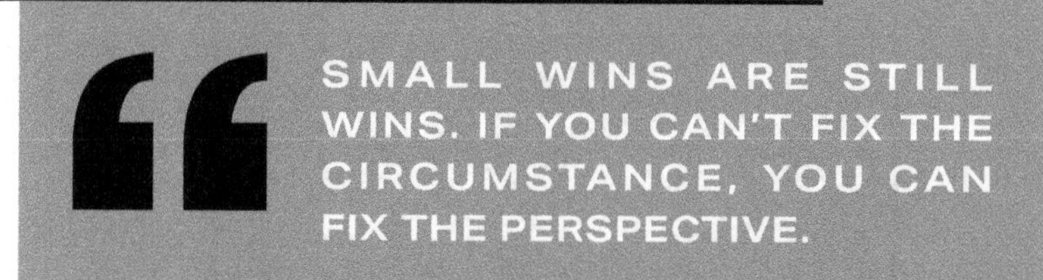

If you're participating in an obstacle course, and you come to your first challenge, do you look at it and say, "Oh. This is too hard, I quit."? No. You think about your options... *How am I going to do this? I can't get around it. I can't climb over it. I can't dig under it. I can't jump that high. I need to get to the next obstacle, so, what are my options? All I can do is take the punishment? Okay. What's the punishment? Ten push-ups? Great. I will do ten push-ups and move on.*

In life, we are way too likely to quit at the first obstacle.

Chris, life isn't an obstacle course.

Fair enough, reader. Maybe life isn't an obstacle course, but life *is* about choices. You will encounter a lot of obstacles in life (kind of like... an obstacle course), and you can only see what you choose to see. If you choose to see an obstacle as a miserable thing, it will be a miserable thing. If you choose to see an obstacle as a game, it will be a game.

I don't care if you have fun or not; I just care that you get through the damn course.

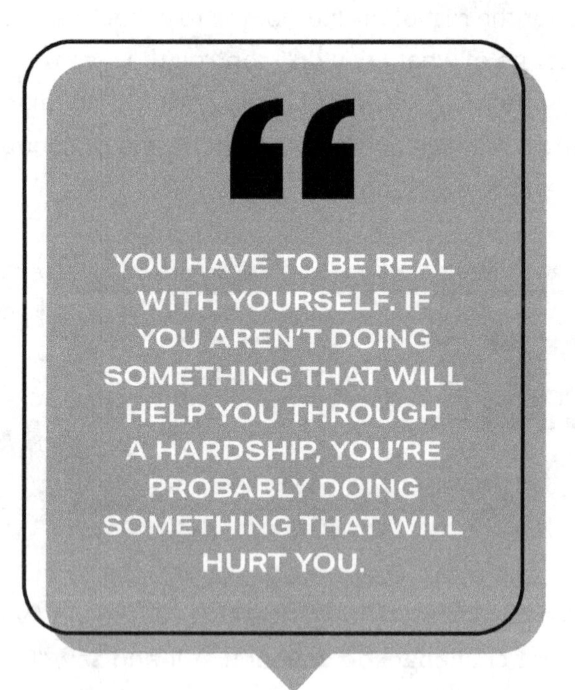

I'm like you: human. I mess up. But I recognize that I am in control of how I look at a situation and that I have choices. It usually goes like this...

Damn, this isn't good. Why am I spiralling? What are my options? What can I do in this situation?

If I'm in a situation where I have to do monkey bars, that is literally impossible for me. I have one hand. I cannot do monkey bars. But I *can* ask what the other options are and do something else, instead. What's the punishment? I'll cut my losses and do that.

In the real world, there might not be a pass. In the real world, you might have to deal with what you can't control and focus on what you can control. Your "punishment" or task will be reframing the obstacle to serve your forward momentum toward success.

If it's something you can't do, focus on what you can do. If you have to pivot, pivot. When a global pandemic happens—an international, universal obstacle—everyone is forced to pivot. Lifestyles and mindsets are flexible. Regardless of the desired outcome, people have to work around what is, and not just live in a fantasy of how they wish things were.

Otherwise, I would be stuck looking at those monkey bars for years, waiting for something to change for me. But I'm not going to grow a new hand.

People get stuck looking at their obstacle, believing they can't do it and complaining about it, instead of taking the temporary loss and moving on to make the further gain.

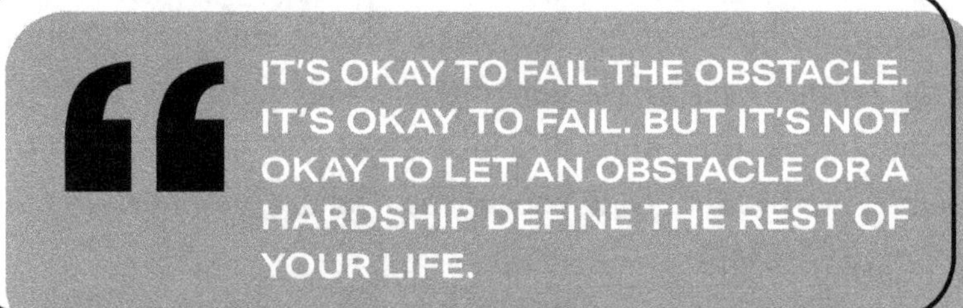

When I was a little kid, I wanted to be a fire truck (yes, a fire truck and not a firefighter). As I got older, I wanted to be a lawyer. If I based where I am now in life on the goals I had in my past, technically, I failed. I'm not a lawyer or a fire truck, to my surprise. We tend to let the shortcomings of our past desires influence our perceived level of success, not only now but indefinitely. Often, if people did not accomplish goals set in the past, they automatically apply that "coming up short" history to their future.

Some people stick to that narrative in their heads for so long that if it doesn't work out how they imagined, life is over. Whether you think life has a plan for you or not, I don't want to argue that. It's your responsibility to do what you are going to do with the hand you were dealt.

Sir James Dyson failed 5,126 times before creating the bagless vacuum cleaner that led to an over 4 billion dollar net worth.

Drew Houston's SAT prep business flopped, but then he went on to create DropBox.

Sara Blakely failed the LSAT twice and moved back in with her parents before creating Spanxx several years later.

Just know that failing is okay. Failing is normal.

There is a huge difference between failing and failure. Failing is a verb. It's something you do, like stubbing your toe or tripping. It happens, and it might sting, and that's completely okay. Failure is a noun. Failure is an identity. Failure is the idea that failing is as far as you'll ever get, so you might as well quit.

Failing is ok. Becoming a failure is not. Not all who fail are failures, but by identifying yourself as a failure, you remove the option to succeed.

To be a failure is to accept that where you are now is final. I don't accept that.

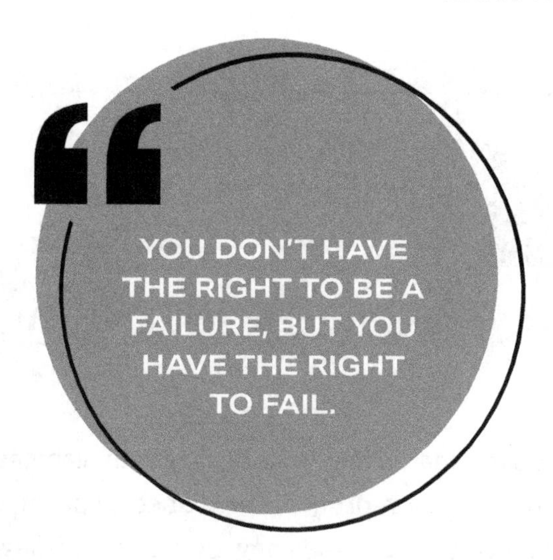

People put so much weight on that word. Remove the emotion from the word and just accept it for what it is. When you can collect those thoughts and remove the emotions that cause your downfall, you can really say, okay, maybe I did mess up. Something happened, but am I a failure because of that? No.

Is the person who stole once a thief for the rest of their life? Are we defining the rest of our lives by one little moment (or a string of moments)? If you choose to, yes. We have so much more control over ourselves than we give ourselves credit for.

I was born with a disability. I was later diagnosed with Type 1 Diabetes. Diabetes became a catalyst to change. I changed my degree program from political science to exercise. I looked at this new obstacle (diabetes) as a game. Working with David, as I shared in **Concept 2**, helped me to see that I had to stop letting my disability define me; when I learned I had diabetes, I decided I was not going to let that break me. I decided to make life the way I wanted it to be, instead of being a victim of my diagnosis.

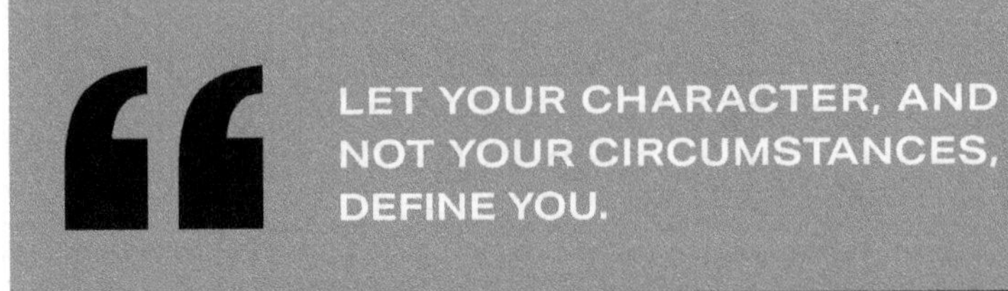

When I publicly shared that I was dealing with diabetes, a friend of mine (who ran a non-profit in the diabetes space) found out and asked if I would do a speaking gig about my diagnosis. I'd always wanted to be a professional speaker, and I was really excited to give it a try. So, I did.

After I left the stage, I knew that everything I'd been through up to that moment had primed me for this opportunity. And it might never have happened for me without getting and accepting that diabetes diagnosis.

From the moment I left the stage, I did every single thing I could to become a better speaker so that my message could be heard. I wanted to help other people. I'd given myself such a hard time for so long. I had told myself the same story, over and over, about how having one hand put me in a losing position. Honestly? Maybe I was in a losing position.

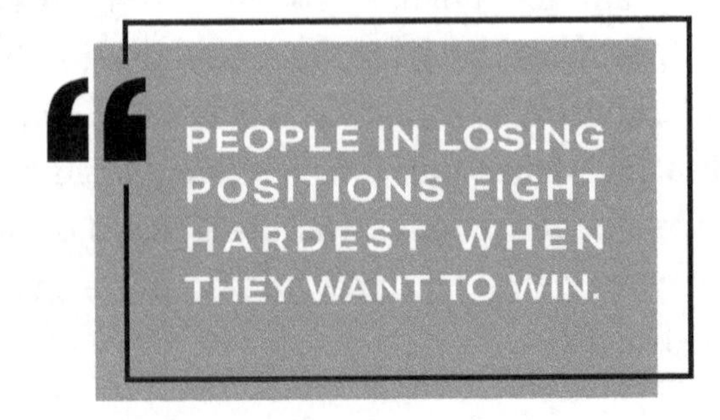

The "when they want to win" part of that sentence is important. You can see this happening in races, when, at the quarter mile point, you see the people in the back either trying to **keep up** or starting to **give up**. They've decided they aren't going to win, so they're done. Then there are the amazing races where you see someone shift and haul ass, going from the back of the pack to the front. Those people receive many cheers. Being at the back is damn hard, but those runners decided not to accept failure. They decided not to accept defeat in the moment and to do something for their future. They want to win, so they go after it.

I felt like diabetes was that for me. It was the kick in the ass I needed to do something about my situation.

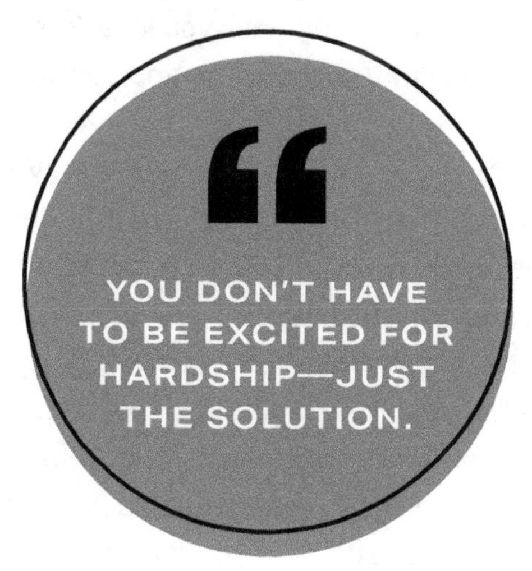

I'm not encouraging you to be excited that your life is a shit show. But I am saying that you aren't entitled to sit back and let yourself lose. Losing from hardship is deciding you have no options. There's always a way through it. If you're still breathing, you are of value. You have a way. There's something you can do.

When some people hear that I have diabetes, they say, "If I had to give myself a shot, I would never do that. I couldn't do it."

Really? Well, I do it because I want to live.

"How do you live with one hand?"

Uh, well, what's my other option?

There's no need to celebrate your hardships, but before you freak out, take a step back and ask yourself, what do I need to do in this position—short or long term—to win?

If your windshield wiper isn't working, you don't take a sledgehammer to the car. So why is it that if you eat one piece of cake, you throw your whole diet out the window? How does that make sense?

We have to start treating our personal problems like real-world problems. We are so good at solving external problems. How do I know this? One of the best ways to solve your own problems is to pretend they belong to someone you love. Pretend someone has come to you with that problem, and consider the advice you'd give them.

When you give advice to someone you love, you genuinely want them to be happy, and you believe they deserve to win. But when that issue is yours, you don't think you deserve the same things. You think you deserve less than them. People you love deserve everything but when it comes to you, it's different. People love giving advice about things they're currently struggling with. It's easy to talk about the things that need to be done; it's hard to do the things that need to be done. **Treat yourself like the person you love, and you'll always have the best advice.** (See the next chapter for more.)

For our internal problems, we focus on quick fixes and things that make us feel better. We want to push responsibility aside. We focus on the why, but this is where the why doesn't matter.

Why the hardship is happening dulls in comparison to why you should break through this hardship. The former question does nothing for you; the latter question gives you internal motivation to figure out what to do because you have a goal in mind. The why of the problem itself isn't going to help. I could consider the why of my disability for the rest of my life, but the rest of my life wouldn't be worth living if I kept focusing on the why. Even if I figured out the why and identified whatever molecule happened to cause my hand to be this way… so what? I still am going to be exactly where I am. What am I going to do about it now?

Hardship sucks. But sometimes you just need a new angle.

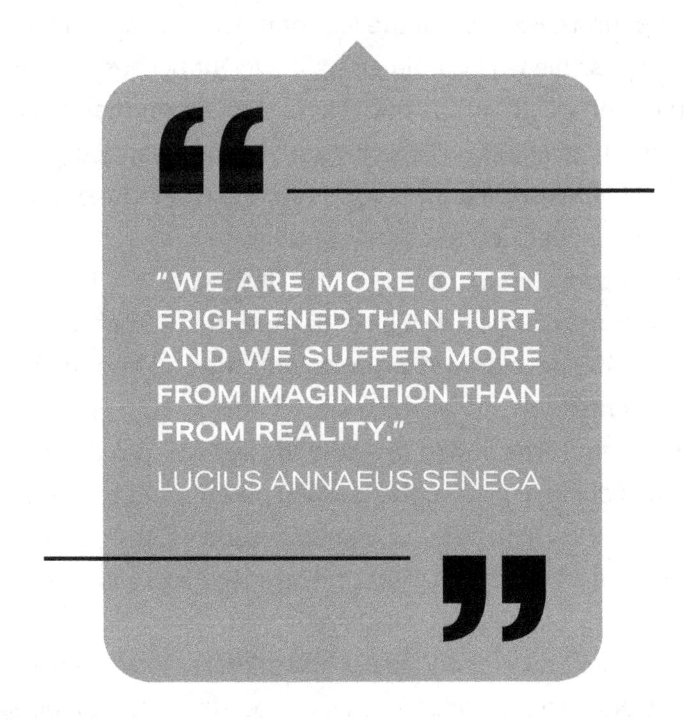

Let me be clear: nobody wants to suffer. But life will involve suffering to some degree. We all get overwhelmed at times. But we aren't allowed to let that overwhelming feeling control the rest of our lives.

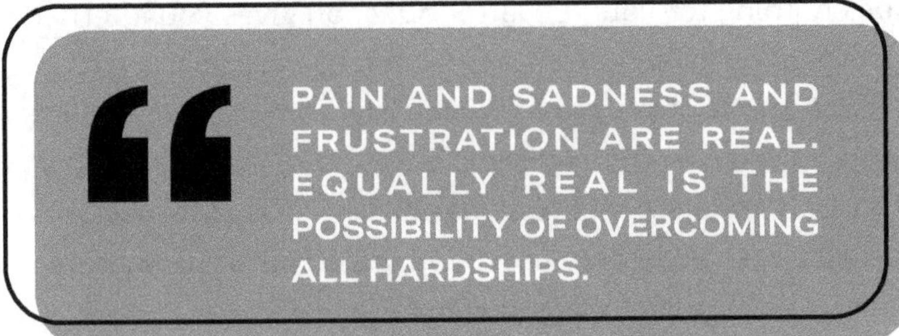

When I first started deadlifting, I could barely lift the bar itself. It's 45 pounds. Because of the lack of function in my arm, there was no possible way I could go up in weight because I couldn't even lift the weight of the bar. It's hard to accept that you can't do something like this. To know you're a one-handed guy in a two-handed world is not a good feeling. But I looked at that obstacle and decided to figure out a way to win.

I developed a hook that helped me lift weights, and I got to the point where I could lift 135 pounds. And then 225 pounds, 315 pounds, 405 pounds, 495 pounds, and then 500 pounds. And the hook held up.

My residual limb ended up red and swollen from the weight, but I was doing it. I got to the low 600 pounds and blood would come out of my limb because of the pressure. I literally had blood coming out of my pores. That's how much I was willing to deal with, to overcome my circumstance.

I didn't look at the 45 pound bar and think, *I can't do this*. I accept the loss. No. I did the work. Did it happen overnight? No. It took eight years. I had the choice to not try, but, I chose to win the moment instead. I chose to make sure I did something before I gave up. Winning doesn't mean against anyone else, but yourself.

I was that runner at the back of the pack. I decided I wanted to win. I tried as many things as I could.

If you tell yourself you've tried everything, and you still continue to lose, you're probably lying to yourself. If you try dieting for a day, that won't work. If you try a new job for a day, you probably won't get a paycheque for a couple of weeks. Trying and doing are very different. You have to be real with yourself. I was real with myself then, and I am today. I'm going to take it upon myself to find a way to make it work. Whether that's staying in the lane I'm in or changing lanes, as long as I'm moving forward... hardship will never be final.

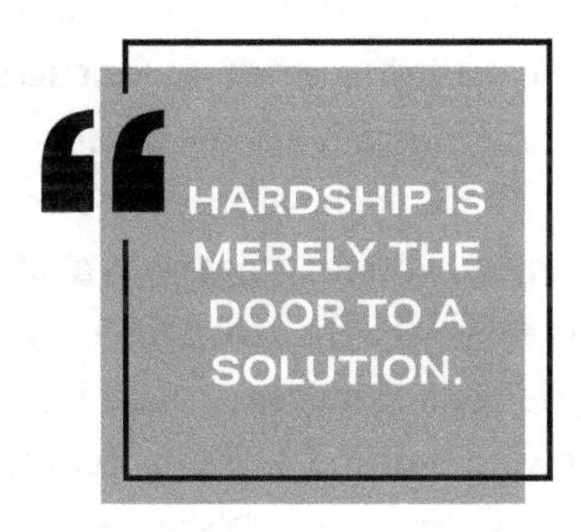

Sometimes the tough stuff seems like the end of the world, but often it's just the beginning. It's easy to be short-sighted because it feels better.

The future continues through your plans... through your ability to stay strong... through obstacles and hardship. You need to remind yourself that this isn't what you want or don't want—this is just what is. Ask yourself, *what can I do through the '**what is**' that can lead to winning and not losing.*

Life is like an escape room. Clues are everywhere; we just stop looking for them and we accept defeat. We accept hardship as a destination. Hardship is not a destination. It's not somewhere you stay—it's somewhere you pass through. This perspective shift helps you overcome the day and win the moment.

Having the upper hand over your struggles is about winning moments. You won't win every single moment, and if, so far in your life, you have won every moment, you have a damn big obstacle coming your way. Financial, emotional, what have you—it's coming. There will be a moment you don't win. I've had hundreds of moments where I didn't win and thousands where I positioned myself to win, and I did win. Don't rely on external positioning to win moments; instead, focus on internal positioning.

Internal positioning starts in your mind. Words are damn loud when you repeat them over and over again. If those words predict your future, are you setting yourself up for success or failure?

Changing your inner narrative takes practise. It's not easy to stop telling yourself those negative stories. I know because I was that person. I told myself everyday that I was a failure. It got to the point where I didn't even need the reminder anymore. I knew I was a failure, so I stopped telling myself. It went from telling myself I sucked to just knowing I sucked. I was content to live, knowing I was a failure. It wasn't until I started recognizing my self-destructive patterns, challenging those thoughts, and changing the way I spoke to, and about, myself, that I started to understand:

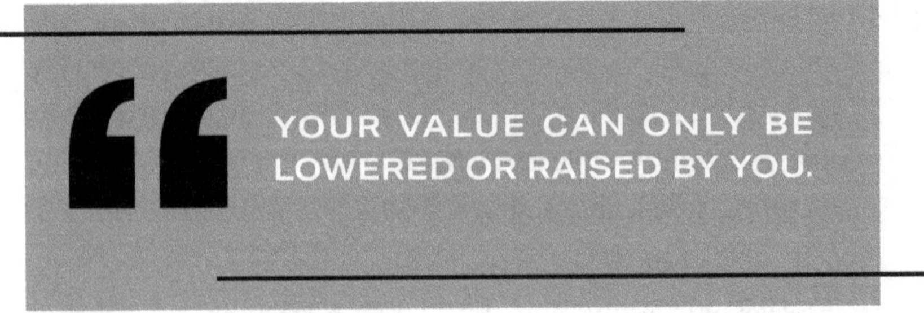

That's the scary part of conditioning. When you condition yourself, that learned helplessness we talked about in Concept 2 comes into play. Some people never get out of that mindset.

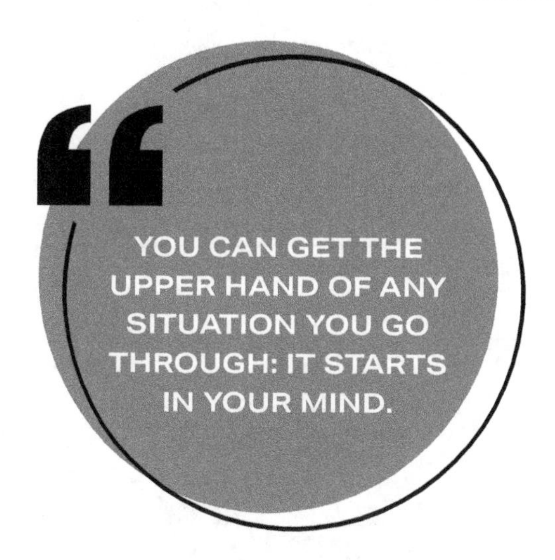

Sometimes it will involve doing something you don't want to do. You may have to make the lower move. That might be leaving a toxic scenario or taking a punishment, but you always have the choice. Stop telling yourself otherwise.

Remember, there's the you who wants to see you fail in comfort, and the you who wants you to succeed through obstacles. It's you versus you. Just make sure the best version of you wins. **Hardship is just a game.**

CONCEPT FIVE:

TREAT YOURSELF LIKE YOUR OWN BEST FRIEND

Imagine your best friend just sent you a text or called you up to say she's feeling miserable. She keeps repeating over and over that she's a failure. She's worthless and completely stuck in her life, and she will never ever be successful.

What would you say to her? Would you tell her that those thoughts are correct? Would you tell her that she's on the right path? Would you tell her those thoughts will lead to her inevitable happiness? I'm willing to bet you wouldn't let her treat herself that way. You would probably try, at the very least, to talk her down and remind her of all the good things in her life. You'd probably explain to her that those thoughts are not only untrue, but will also not put her in a position to win. You would probably even go out of your way to find every positive, effective, and reinforcing thought that you can come up with to make the situation better for her.

Now, how about that negative self-talk that goes through your own head on repeat: Why can't you have the same kind of compassion for yourself as you would for a friend?

It's easier to help other people than it is to help yourself. It feels good to give advice to other people because you don't have to go through the pain and struggle yourself.

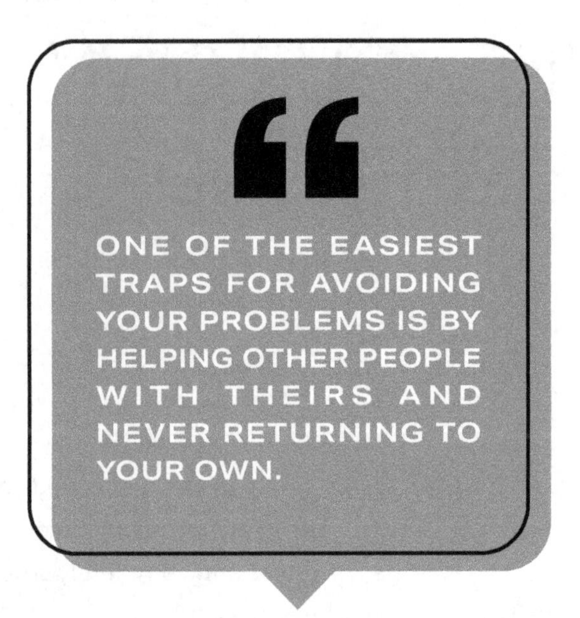

If that friend calls you up crying because of how she is sucking at life, are you going to say, "Yeah, you do suck. You're a shitty person, and nothing is ever going to get any better." Of course not! But we do it all the time when we talk to ourselves. You tell yourself things you would never EVER say to someone you love.

Why are we so willing to break ourselves down, but we go out of our way to build other people up?

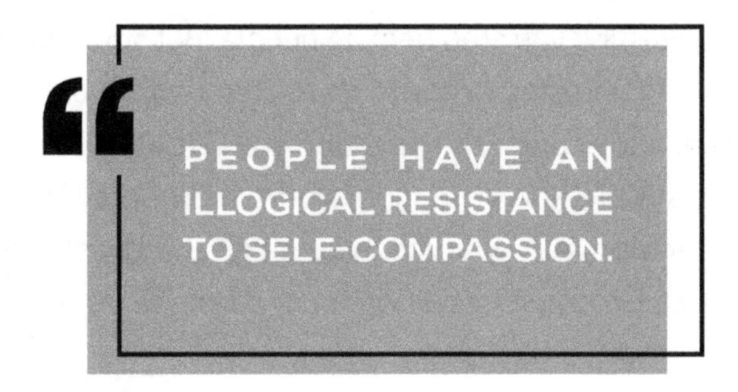

We believe other people deserve compassion, but we don't. It's because we see their highlight reels. A small commercial of their lives. The parts they want us to see on social media. And we judge ourselves on those. It's cherry picking a viewpoint on someone else's life that you're creating in your head. You have this whole facade in place of why you suck and they don't. You have put in so much time and effort... a huge investment in why you suck. But the second someone else has the same problem, you have ten reasons ready to help them and a guide book on how they can get out of their bad situation.

I've done this tons of times. Part of the reason I got into speaking was that it was the best way to not deal with my own issues. I was still hiding my disability while teaching people to be confident. I seemed confident, so people believed me. I hid my lack of confidence in confidence. I subconsciously made people think I was confident. Look at him! He's on stage. If he wasn't confident, he wouldn't be there. **I was literally hiding my hand in front of thousands of people.**

There's a quote I heard once that I will never forget: you teach best what you need to learn most.

I hid what I taught people not to hide, until I figured out I needed to stop hiding. Then, I shared that journey with them, too. You're not wrong to try and help people overcome something.

I'm not suggesting you stop helping people. But start helping you, too. We can't skip step one and go to step two. If you do skip it, come back and answer the question you left blank.

Try this simple line of reasoning the next time you have to make a decision. Ask yourself, would I give my best friend this same advice I'm giving myself right now? *Um, no, it's shitty advice*. Okay, then that's a bad idea.

We can identify when advice is bad when we're dishing it out to someone else, but we take our own bad advice over and over. Until we can learn to domesticate emotions through the right questions, we keep doing this. You have to learn to domesticate your emotions in a way that doesn't determine your demise.

What is this idea of domesticating emotion?

It's talked about in stoicism. There's a belief among people that you have to become emotionless to be logical. An emotionless robot. But that's not true. Domesticating emotion means controlling emotion, so it does not control you, putting you in the position to make a logical move against whatever hardship you're facing.

Any war that was won was not won based on emotion; yet, emotions were had. Emotions are a very real part of dealing with adversity or any circumstances. But if you cannot control your emotions, and, instead, you let them control you, you are reacting instead of responding. And all decisions made from that point are made on a rocky foundation.

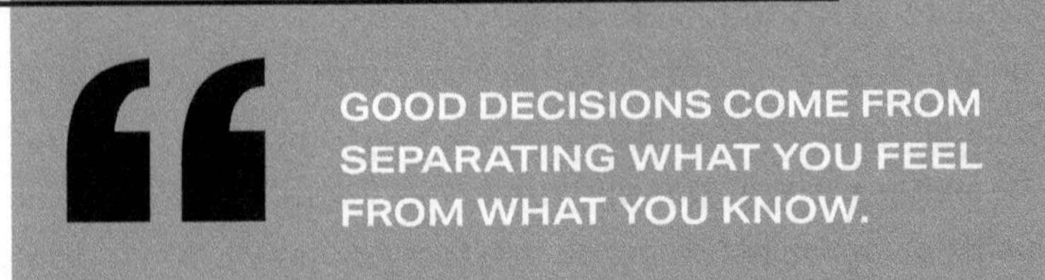

Would I treat someone I love this way? No. Why? Because I love them. Do I love myself? If not, why? Am I judging myself based on a few scenarios? Do my past actions dictate my future character? No. Okay. I have the right to be happy, and I should love myself so I treat myself the way I would a loved one.

If you see someone standing outside crying, you will likely have a basic human reaction. Even if you don't want to get involved, you probably feel sad for them. There is a sense of interconnectedness between humans. People want to help other people.

That sense of compassion is lost when applied to ourselves.

I was in an airport once, on an important call. There was a woman crying, across from me. She was very upset, and she was alone. I stood up, passed her some napkins, and made eye contact. I didn't feel the need to hang up the phone and ask her what was wrong. I just wanted to show her that I saw her and wanted to help. Human compassion. The smallest gestures matter. If you apply that kind love to yourself, so many little problems would be a lot less terrible. Not that they would go away, but we would be better suited to deal with them.

A lot of our suffering comes from the way we treat ourselves and talk to ourselves about the problems we are currently facing. But the problems we face have no emotion except for the emotion we give them. We choose to apply emotion to emotionless circumstances. And while it is a natural human response to have emotions, it is our responsibility to domesticate them.

There was a time in my life where I was convinced that other people deserved more happiness than me. You have to realize that nobody is better or worse than anyone else. If someone else can achieve happiness, you can too.

> WE ALL HAVE EQUAL POTENTIAL. MAYBE THE STARTING POSITION IS DIFFERENT, BUT YOU ALWAYS HAVE THE POTENTIAL TO DO YOUR BEST, GIVEN YOUR CIRCUMSTANCES.

There have been people who started in last place and finished first. And vice versa. It's willpower. It's choosing to do what you can with where you are and choosing to get up if you fall. You have to choose to work harder, regardless of where you start from.

The problem is that people see a certain starting position as indefinite failure, so they don't even try. It once again goes back to learned helplessness. People tend to take a screenshot of where they are or where they came from and then copy and paste that across the rest of their life. They apply their current or past circumstances to their future, never allowing themselves to be better than what they've had or what they currently are.

> DON'T MIRROR YOUR FUTURE LIFE TO YOUR PAST LIFE — A LIFE THAT HASN'T EVEN HAPPENED YET. GIVE YOURSELF A CHANCE TO BECOME YOUR FUTURE SELF AND NOT JUST A CARBON COPY OF YOUR PAST.

It is unfair and illogical to accept and apply current circumstances to your future potential. And, again, you would never do this to someone you love. You'd never say to a family member going through addiction, "You're going to be a drug addict for the rest of your life, so you might as well just go buy some more drugs." Because you know that is a dooming thought and prediction.

But, to yourself, you're okay saying, "Oh well, yeah, this is destructive behaviour, but I'm a lost cause so I'm going to keep doing it anyway."

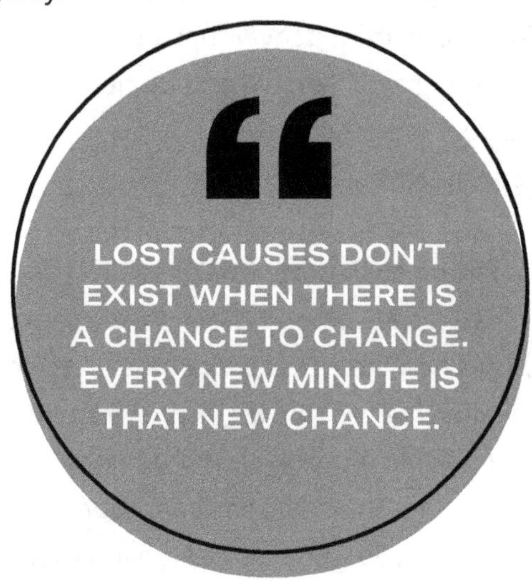

How many people were told they were lost causes (by themselves or others) and became the biggest cause? Helen Keller was born blind and deaf but became an author nominated for a Nobel Prize. She wasn't even able to speak, but everybody knows her name. Jay-Z, a hip hop artist turned business mogul, was turned down by every record label and told he was terrible before creating his own label, leading to chart-topping hits and over a billion dollar net worth. Harrison Ford was told he would never make it as an actor and should just quit. Fifty movies later, including the iconic Star Wars franchise, I'd say he and many others were never lost causes.

Why was I okay telling myself to keep on spiralling when I would walk someone else out of the same situation?

You'll help someone else through a problem by giving them a step-by-step plan, if they ask for it. Why not do that for yourself? We'll say to ourselves, *you suck*. But that's not how you help someone or teach someone. It's not how you fix something. You might have no clue about cars, but if you know you have a flat tire, you don't just leave it. You don't just walk away and never go back to the car. But when we have a personal problem, we will set it aside and plan to deal with it later. "It's not bothering me right now," we'll say. Then, we end up never addressing it.

Excuse me, your tire is going flat.

"Nah, I have an air bubble, it's fine."

Over time, it gets worse and worse, and the worst part is that it's gotten so bad on such a minimal level that you adapt to it. The new worse isn't the same as the old worse—it's just worse.

We adapt to this new increased "worstness"—an increased terribleness—and tell ourselves that it's okay. We knew a month ago, a year ago, that we had a problem. But until the tire blows, we'll ignore it. Until you get in an accident and hurt people because of your problem that you said was okay, even though you knew you needed to fix it. You see someone else with a flat tire, you go out of your way to make sure they fix it. Why? Resistance to self-compassion.

There's some truth to the saying that suggests, "those who can't do, teach." There are bodybuilder coaches who have never been bodybuilders. There are people coaching NFL teams who have never played in the NFL. We can learn about problems so much that we give advice rather than take it. Not to take away from anyone who has a knowledge base to draw from—a doctor can tell people about diabetes without having it—but by not taking your own advice, you're either showing that advice is not sound, or that you don't think you're worth fixing.

I could go into the psychology of confidence and not practicing what I preach. If I help people, that's okay. But if I'm going home unhappy at the end of the day, that's on me. That's building other people's houses and having the tools to build myself the best house; yet, I'm sleeping in a tent. You had every resource you needed, but you didn't make a decision to treat yourself the way you treat other people. You decided to not treat yourself the way you would treat someone you care about.

You decide other people are more important or that you're less important. It's not nice to feel like crap about yourself. It makes life so much harder. But, somehow, in our minds, there is a safety net around feeling terrible about yourself. There's a release of responsibility when you feel bad about yourself. When you believe you're a loser and that you'll never amount to anything. That life is against you. By thinking those things, it relieves you of your responsibility to ever make something of yourself. You can't fail at something you don't do. If you never drive, you won't crash your car into someone else's. If you don't fall in love, you can't get hurt. That is a protective mechanism—a sense of insecurity and a safety net against getting hurt. A net against responsibility.

People are so afraid of not achieving a goal that they won't even try. But you would never say to a niece or nephew, "Oh, you want to be a dancer? Too bad. You're going to be a grocery bagger forever and hate your life. You're probably going to be addicted to cigarettes and alcohol and be alone forever."

That is an awful prediction, but it's the inner monologue of most people who are negative or self-deprecating. And we only see it as a problem when we say it to someone else. That is how ineffective our brains are.

It's simple, but it's not easy. And the hard part is that you have to think about this on a minute-by-minute basis. Everyone likes doing the right thing when the right thing is the easiest thing.

But when something bad happens to you, you don't want to be motivational. It's hard when you're having a dark moment to treat yourself well. Just try to ask yourself, "Am I treating myself like someone I love?"

You have to ask yourself that question whenever you're talking to yourself about important things like your goals. This will help you make sure your thoughts and reactions and responses are effective. If they aren't, you aren't treating yourself like someone you love. You have to catch that and say, "Nope that thought isn't allowed. That's not a thought I want to continue having." As quick as it pops up, you have to squash it.

People say communication is key. But they often skip the most important aspect of communication, which is **self-communication.**

You talk to yourself more than you talk to anyone else, and you're also the person you put the least amount of effort into understanding. How you talk to yourself dictates your choices and how you respond to struggle. How you talk to yourself influences how you communicate with others. And not only that, but how you talk to yourself influences how you view yourself and how others view you. People will view you the same way you view yourself.

Even people who try to become better communicators skip self-communication. We never even consider the way we communicate with ourselves, and we go straight to communicating with others. But self-communication creates your own belief system, whether good or bad. **You can predict your own defeat, or you can tell yourself you can get through anything.**

When you're faced with struggle, you can get the upper hand via the way you self-communicate. It's all about perception. You can be the person who has the high ground by self-communication tactics you've already developed prior to the problem, or you can be the person who reacts to the problem, scrambling to put yourself together. **The latter option puts you at a disadvantage, not because of the problem itself, but because of what you did prior to the problem.**

You have to expect the chaos. For the flat tire to come (because it will). And more importantly than that, you have to know how not to turn a flat tire into a self-destructive character analysis of why your life sucks and how the universe hates you. You need to be proactive with self-communication. Get that belief system in place before a struggle comes your way. The way we communicate with ourselves provides the foundation for our house. But we usually don't consider this until things start to crack.

If a problem arises, make sure your communication strategies are not casting stones at your character as well. There's no need to inflame hardship with self-sabotage.

This gets easier and more effective over time. You can't play tennis once, then go to Wimbledon. You can't just drive fast, then go to Nascar. You have to become good at self-communicating, and you only become good if you practise. It only becomes effective if you practise. The easiest way to evaluate how you're being is to put someone in your shoes and give them advice. Ask yourself how you would help them, and then do that for yourself.

CONCEPT SIX:

HAVE THE UPPER HAND

According to Greek mythology, Zeus got fed up of Sisyphus' deceitful ways and dealt him a punishment: to push a huge boulder up a hill of Hades for all of eternity. Most people would say that's a bad thing. But I feel like Sisyphus was in a beneficial position because every single day he started a seemingly impossible task; then he finished it. He completed it and would have the sense of getting it done.

Obviously, life is supposed to be better than that, but, to me, that boulder epitomizes the idea of overcoming yourself every single day.

People have a negative connotation of pushing a boulder up a hill. But life is full of hills and peaks and valleys. Some days, you'll have to push a rock up a hill. Some days, you'll have to hold it back from rolling down on you. Being able to push that rock up fills you with pride, and falling down with it teaches humility. You will have to dig yourself out, rise up, and try to keep yourself at the peaks. **It all comes down to how you choose to think about the rock.**

Whether your circumstances are good, bad, or ugly (or anything in between), you're never powerless. Even if you're in a situation like Sisyphus. There's never a time when you can't do something or think something differently. You can always take a moment to put yourself in a position of advantage.

Clearly, none of us want to be Sisyphus. But because Sisyphus was given no option other than to push the rock up the hill, he, like many of us, had to choose how to interpret his circumstances. Like him, we often have to interpret circumstances that we can't change so that we can extract a sense of satisfaction and quality of life even in the most unpleasant of scenarios.

Throughout this book, we've covered how the biggest problems come from what we perceive in a situation and how we react, rather than respond. Now it's up to you to take time to respond to each situation appropriately. To value yourself enough to not be affected by the things that happen to you or by you or from you. By having the upper hand over yourself, you have the upper hand over your thoughts. You have the ability to go between negative thoughts and the potential to find a solution.

I don't want you getting to this point of the book thinking, *Hey! Now I can manipulate anyone! Nothing will ever hurt me.* I promise you, that's wrong. If you read this book, you'll still get hurt at some point because that's life. But, after reading this book, you'll be able to take any situation that happens and think through a lens that turns adversity to advantage. To leverage so-called limitations and look at them in a way that will predict your success rather than your failure.

Andy Frisella was a dirt road kid that society painted as a nobody. He worked painting the lines in parking lots, he slept on a used piss-stained mattress in the back of a business that wasn't turning a profit, he was brutally attacked in the face with a knife for standing up to racists, he was robbed, vandalized, and disrespected. He had every reason to quit.

It took over eight years, but he built a business from nothing to revenues topping 100 million dollars that would lead him to being named an Inc. 500 entrepreneur.

Andy epitomizes the idea of gaining the upper hand over yourself at times that matter most. And he's influenced millions of lives because of his ability to leverage his limitations and turn his adversity into advantage.

STOP FANTASIZING ABOUT FAILING, AND START ACCEPTING THE POSSIBILITY OF CHANGE, SUCCESS, AND THAT YOU COULD WIN EVERY MOMENT REGARDLESS OF YOUR POSITION.

To help you get the advantage over your inner self saboteur gives me hope for this book and this concept and humanity in general.

The quality of your life is determined by your outlook. And not just your outlook when things are good—it's also determined by your outlook when things go wrong. What are your most common thoughts? Are you at the bottom or the top of the hill in your own mind? Are you fighting an uphill battle? Are you Sisyphus?

This book does not contain shocking or revolutionary information. When you think better, you start feeling better, reacting better, and surrounding yourself with better people. You make better decisions to better your day and to better your life.

When you start thinking better, life starts getting better because you have the upper hand over the one thing you can control: you.

"Yeah, Chris, that sounds nice. But it's easier said than done."

To me, that is a false narrative that is easily accepted. When it seems like everything you've wanted is failing, your reality is going against the story you've told yourself. *I need this, and if I don't have it, I will not be happy*. That's such a black and white lie we tell ourselves to never have the upper hand.

You are the marble and the sculptor. You cause yourself the pain, but you also deliver yourself from the pain. As humans, we have a false narrative of what we want life to be.

If what we see doesn't agree with the narrative, we're unhappy.

If what we see agrees with the narrative, we are happy.

It's the valleys and peaks. When the rock has to be stopped and you're holding yourself on that hill... yeah, life isn't going your way at that moment, and you have to take a step back.

Life just goes in a certain way, and you have to position yourself around that rock.

Having the upper hand doesn't sound sexy. It's not meant to be sexy. I'm not trying to Disney-fy this. You're not a comic book hero. You can't shoot webs out of your wrists or fly or wear red and black tights and be a jackass who makes corny comebacks. But you have control over your thoughts. To metaphorically cut the negative ones out of your mind.

By choosing to metaphorically use a scalpel to remove the negative thoughts and feelings from your mind, taking out those bits that slowly ruin you, you give yourself peace of mind and put yourself in a position to win, mentally.

Enough peace of mind gives you quality of life—a solid foundation to make a decision upon. If you're balancing on one leg on a tiny, two-inch wooden pole, there's no way that when life throws things at you that you can jump, dodge, or pivot without falling. Your whole life will be spent balancing on this tiny foundation where you have no way to make a change. By increasing your quality of life, you expand your foundation so you can use your one foot effectively. You have more ground to cover, and now you can make a proper decision to dodge, duck, dip, dive, and dodge, repositioning yourself around the problems that happen.

Whether we cause our own problems or they stem from external sources (many times we cause our own problems, FYI), it's still our responsibility to protect and improve our mentality so we can be flexible around life, which is often inflexible. Negating this philosophy only negates your potential happiness and your possibility to control what little you can control.

Our society is so obsessed with getting the upper hand over external circumstances. We want the upper hand over the person we're selling to, our partner, our children... We always want control. But we only want to control things that are not us.

We are so obsessed with outside circumstances, but we are scared to put that same effort toward ourselves. It's okay if someone else lets us down—we're used to that. But the thought of letting ourselves down is inconceivable, stopping us from even attempting the things that might better our lives. When it comes to changing the way you think, it's easier to blame someone else, rather than take responsibility.

When you reach the end of this book, nobody is going to clap for you and praise you for starting to think better. Like the person who runs the race and gets to the finish line an hour after everyone has left, you have to be proud of yourself and your actions, knowing that you did something significant.

The quality of your life is determined by the quality of your thoughts, and that is all in your head. Everything is internal. Some people rely on external circumstances (applause) to stimulate internal feelings of worthiness or accomplishment, as reminded by the applause. It's all in your head. It's great to receive external congratulations, but no amount of praise or support matters if you aren't proud of who you are and who you are becoming.

This book is about character. About who you are behind closed doors. You won't get likes for changing your mindset on social media. It involves you calling yourself out. If something hurts you, you can help yourself. If you don't help yourself, you're letting it hurt you. It's you versus you here. And you don't get a reward. It's like doing chores—you know you need to do them, and if you don't, you're only adding hardship to your life. The good thoughts are not rewarded but the bad thoughts are penalized with a lower quality of life and a feeling of being out of control. Having the upper hand over yourself is a necessity to live your best life. You can change your circumstances, even if it is just changing your narrative.

No abs, cars, or relationships will help you if you're in a position to fail everyday. I lived that lifestyle for almost two decades. And what I realized was that once you decide to have the upper hand over the thoughts, beliefs, and actions that hurt you, you realize the pain only comes from yourself and that **quality of life is only achieved through internal thoughts, not external things**. That's when you can make your life better. You have to have the upper hand over yourself.

You have to self-communicate. To turn the things in your life that you perceive as bad into better things. If you're not bettering your life, you're making it worse. Stagnation is not improvement. You'll never look back and think, *Oh yay, I was stagnant*.

Lack of progress in any department of life can make people feel depressed or devalued. Progress does not require extreme success. Progress can simply be choosing an effective thought over an ineffective thought.

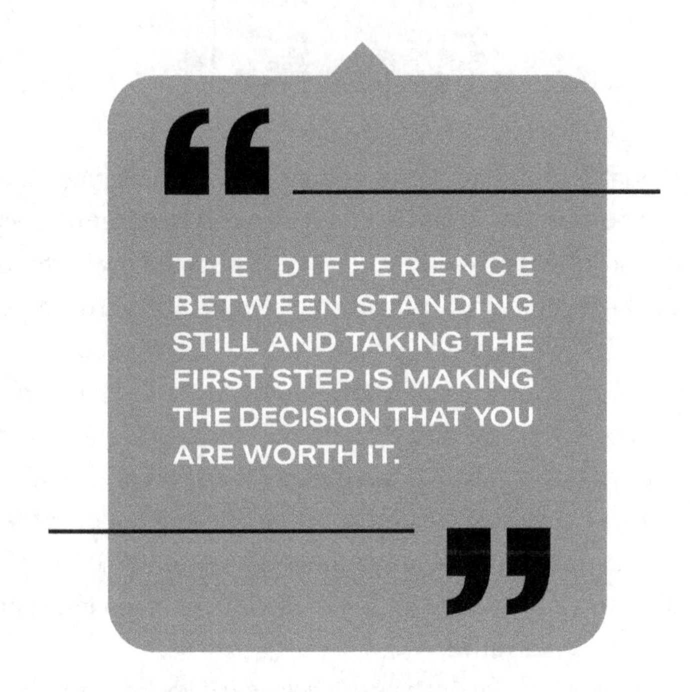

Having the upper hand over yourself is a concept meant to help you **in the moment, win the moment**, and to have a better life as a result.

ABOUT THE AUTHOR

Chris Ruden is an international keynote speaker, elite powerlifter, entrepreneur, disabled model, and advocate. Despite having been born with only two fingers on his left hand and a shorter left arm, he can deadlift over 675 pounds and is on track to become the World's strongest adaptive athlete.

At nineteen years of age, Chris was diagnosed with Type 1 Diabetes, and while it took time to accept his disease, it's that diagnosis he credits for his career in speaking. On stages (and screens) worldwide, Chris speaks about diversity, inclusion, and overcoming adversity.

Through his humorous, logical, and passionate presentations, Chris uses his struggle to inspire thousands of people to overcome the difficulties they may face in their lives. Now his book, *The Upper Hand*, gives readers the simple tools they need to turn any perceived adversity into an advantage.

While Chris has a bachelor's degree and a list of fitness, therapy, and life coaching certifications (and appeared on The Rock's TV Show, *Titan Games*), his career highlights include helping an 11-year-old with cerebral palsy to walk and an 85-year-old woman beat cancer (twice). Chris is an advocate for fitness, managing diabetes, and the power of a positive mindset in overcoming any limitation.

THE NO BS ALLOWED LIST

Stop looking at hardships as the end of the world, and view them as a game to win.

Stop limiting your potential by the cage you've built around yourself.

Focus on what matters—what you can control.

When you catch yourself saying any of the following things, you are wrong:

I have to ___________________.

You've got yourself convinced that you have do this or you have to do that, but that's bullshit. It's not true. You have a choice. You might not like the options, but you always have options. See page 24.

I'm a failure.

Failing doesn't make you a failure. See page 66.

I've tried everything, and nothing works.

Did you really try everything and commit to it fully each and every time? I don't buy it. See page 73.

I don't have time to _________________.

Really? We all have the same amount of time—we just choose to spend it differently.

I have no choice.

Are you sure about that? Because if you're alive, I beg to differ. (And if you're reading this and you're not alive, you should have a Ted Talk or something.) See page 24.

RUDENISMS

The struggles we will inevitably face can serve to strengthen us.

Focusing on what you cannot control is a losing strategy.

Focusing on the *why* limits you to the past. Focusing on the *what* (as in what you can do about it) creates endless possibilities for the future.

Misery often comes not from what we are going through, but how we *perceive* what we are going through.

The quality of your life depends on the quality of your thoughts. You may not be able to gain the upper hand over outside circumstances, but you can always gain the upper hand over yourself.

When your perspective of *what is* gets pitted against your perspective of *what should be*, it will be impossible to live a good life.

Do not become the victim of your own perspective.

I give no value to what I can't control and only value what I can control.

Who you have been until this point doesn't limit who you can be right now and moving forward.

The desire for change without action creates a cage.

Past failures have no bearing on future successes. The only things that have any bearing on your future are your present behaviours and habits.

You will never get the upper hand over a situation if you don't get the upper hand over yourself first.

The first thing you can do right now to change your life is to think differently.

Your goals are defined by what you do and not what you say you want to do.

You can't get better at playing basketball by practicing tennis. Your actions have to align with your goals.

We stay in relationships that hurt or jobs that suck because we fear the unknown so much that we develop an acquired taste for the pain we're used to, to avoid venturing toward the threat of pain that we don't know.

Just because you've always done something doesn't make it right.

Question every thought or pattern, and ask yourself, *is this helping me or hurting me?* That's how you develop awareness.

Would you rather fail at something new or hurt at something old?

What are the destructive thoughts I'm having that are taking me away from the life I want to live?

Your circumstances don't decide your destiny.

Hardship doesn't guarantee success, and it doesn't guarantee failure.

When you mix in choice, hardship can be either the fuel that pushes you forward or the place where your story ends.

Hardship can destroy your current world so your future world *can* exist.

What's the point in choosing a losing perspective when you have the option to win? Treat hardship like a game.

Small wins are still wins. If you can't fix the circumstance, you can fix the perspective.

You have to be real with yourself. If you aren't doing something that will help you through a hardship, you're probably doing something that will hurt you.

It's okay to fail the obstacle. It's okay to fail. But it's not okay to let an obstacle or a hardship define the rest of your life.

You don't have the right to be a failure, but you have the right to fail.

Let your character, and not your circumstances, define you.

People in losing positions fight hardest when they want to win.

You don't have to be excited for hardship—just the solution.

Pain and sadness and frustration are real. Equally real is the possibility of overcoming all hardships.

Hardship is merely the door to a solution.

Your value can only be lowered or raised by you.

You can get the upper hand of any situation you go through: it starts in your mind.

One of the easiest traps for avoiding your problems is to help other people with theirs and never return to your own.

People have an illogical resistance to self-compassion.

Good decisions come from separating what you feel from what you know.

We all have equal potential. Maybe the starting position is different, but you always have the potential to do your best, given your circumstances.

Don't mirror your future life to your past life — a life that hasn't even happened yet. Give yourself a chance to become your future self and not just a carbon copy of your past.

Lost causes don't exist when there is a chance to change. Every new minute is that new chance.

Treat yourself like someone you're responsible for helping.

Life is better when you think better.

Stop fantasizing about failing, and start accepting the possibility of change, success, and that you could win every moment regardless of your position.

Is it easier said than done? Yes. But it's also better done than said.

Make yourself proud.

The difference between standing still and taking the first step is making the decision that you are worth it.

NEXT CHAPTER PRESS

We create books that help people through life's transitions.

We all face changes, transitions, and life-altering experiences during the story of our life. From celebrations to tragedies, some chapters are joyful and exciting, while others are sad and challenging.

If you are turning a page in your life, we hope our books will be a source of comfort, strength, and inspiration. Written by people who have been through what you're experiencing or have helped others along a similar path, our books will help you move forward with experiences shared, lessons learned, and wisdom gained.

Everyone's story contains many chapters. We hope our books accompany you during this next stage of your life and help make it as meaningful as possible.

An Imprint of Blue Moon Publishers